SPROUTS

by

Harriet Hope Green
Dr. Sue Gillespie Martin

illustrated by Gerald Melton

Cover by Gerald Melton

Copyright © Good Apple, Inc. 1981

ISBN No. 0-86653-028-2

Printing No. 987654321

GOOD APPLE, INC.
BOX 299
CARTHAGE, IL 62321

DEDICATIONS

Sue Gillespie Martin dedicates this book to her father, James Leo Gillespie, for filling her childhood cup with sweet imaginative possibilities.

Harriet Hope Green gives special thanks to Annette, Max and Larry.

THE SENSORY DOOR TO CREATIVITY

Introductory Thoughts
Part I

The sensory system is the door to all perception, understanding, learning and creativity. It has a direct passageway to the brain where the information gathered is processed.

If the sensory door is wide open a child can see, hear, taste, touch and smell the world around him. If this door is only half open he can only experience fifty percent of his world. And if it is shut he is closed off from the development of his human potential.

Part One is designed to make every student aware of the sights, sounds and smells around him by asking him to explore his environment via his mouth, hands, eyes, nose and ears.

Eyes see shape, color, size, brightness and movement. More nerve cells are involved with the visual sense than any of the other senses. The visual sense is the one sense most relied upon today. Eighty percent of our information comes to us through the visual.

Ears are capable of hearing timbre, pitch, volume and rhythm. Unfortunately, with increasing noise pollution ears have been forced to block out much of the auditory world. At the same time ears become insensitive to the beautiful noise - the full spectrum of notes, the multi-shaded expressions of tone color and the lighter patterns of tempo.

The 9,000 taste buds are capable of distinguishing four qualities - sweet, sour, salty, and bitter. The sense of taste along with smell is present at birth.

The most primitive sense is the olfactory, the sense of smell. Prehistoric man relied upon his ability to distinguish smell in order to find food and avoid danger. In fact, in today's world man is still very dependent on his sniffer. The seven basic types of scents are musty (mold), floral (gardenia), ethereal (nail polish), pungent (lemon), putrid (rotten eggs), pepperminty (peppermint Life-savers), and camphoraceous (Vicks).

Texture, size, shape, spatial arrangement, weight, temperature, pressure and pain can all be felt by receptors in the skin. Human hands with their short fingers and long opposable thumbs give man the most versatile tool for touching, gripping, and manipulating objects that evolution has ever seen.

Backyard Games

SEEING WHAT'S THERE

OBJECTIVE: To develop visual awareness of whole pictures as it relates to details.

MATERIALS: Picture of "Backyard Games."

PROCEDURE: 1. Show the class "Backyard Games." Tell them there are fourteen games depicted in the picture. Ask them to find the following games:

LOCATION

1.	Leapfrog	lower right-hand corner
2.	Marbles	right-hand side of picture
3.	Hobby Horse	upper half of picture in the center
4.	Swinging	upper right-hand side
5.	Crack the Whip	center of the picture
6.	Walking on Stilts	lower left-hand corner
7.	Playing with Dolls	lower half in front of bush
8.	Tug-of-War	just above the center of picture
9.	Swinging on a Branch	upper left-hand corner of picture
10.	Riding a Barrel	lower half of center of picture
11.	Balancing a Broom	upper left-hand side of picture
12.	Doing a Headstand	lower half just right of center
13.	Paper Plane Flying	center of the left-hand side of the picture
14.	Fence Walking	upper half of picture just left of center

2. This activity could be followed by a visual study of Bruegel's painting entitled *Children's Games.* There are over fifty-five games depicted.

3. *Find the Cat* by Elaine Livermore (Houghton-Mifflin, 1973) is an excellent book for visual awareness of details. Grades 2-6 will enjoy finding the cat on each page.

PEEPHOLE GUESS

OBJECTIVE: To develop the ability to visualize what the whole object or picture may be by seeing only a part of the object or picture.

MATERIALS: Set of pictures, cover sheets to expose only a portion of each picture, and the book *Look Again* by Tana Hoban (Macmillan, 1971).

PROCEDURE: 1. Have children sit in a semi-circle in front of you very close.

2. Hold up each of the partial pictures from *Look Again* or this book and ask them what they think the whole picture could be. Allow everyone to have a guess before showing the whole picture.

3. This could also be done with real objects and a section of a sheet with a small peephole cut in it. Objects, which could be used are a grapefruit, golf ball, sponge, roll of toilet paper, etc.

4. Children may wish to develop their own peephole guess games or sets of partial pictures.

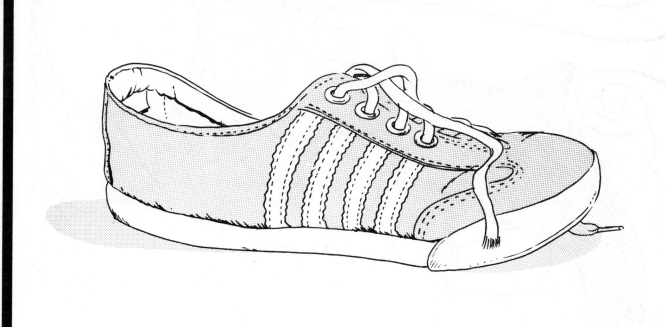

Sea Urchins

STYROFOAM CUP CUTOUTS

OBJECTIVE: To develop visual awareness of shape distinction.

MATERIALS: 12 styrofoam cups, a cutting tool, a stopwatch, colored paper, paste, scissors, white paper and paper cutout entitled "Sea Urchins."

PROCEDURE: 1. Cut the top of each cup from the bottom making different jagged edges as well as different proportions of tops to bottoms.

 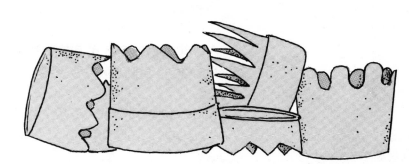

2. Mix up the tops and bottoms and put each of the twenty-four pieces out in a jumble.

3. Have each child attempt to match the tops and the bottoms to form 12 completely fitted cups. The child with the best time is the winner.

4. Have each student take a sheet of colored paper and cut it up into strips, circles, rectangles; whatever shapes happen to result is fine. Then have each mix his shapes into a scattered pile. Ask each student to sift through his pile and reconstruct his original piece of colored paper.

5. Show the class the paper cutout entitled "Sea Urchins." Discuss the shapes and what they stand for in the print. Do you see a fish? What about seaweed? Are there any sharks? Do you see any killer whales?

6. Have students draw their own sea urchins on colored paper, cut them out, arrange them on a piece of paper and paste them in place.

CIRCLES ALL AROUND

OBJECTIVE: To develop an awareness of circle shapes in our lives.

MATERIALS: A pencil and a circle sheet for each player.

PROCEDURE: 1. Have children sit in a large circle.

2. Ask them to look around the room and tell you all the circle shapes they see.

3. Ask them to look at each other and their own clothes and tell you all the circle shapes they see.

4. Pass out circle sheets to students and ask them to make things out of the basic circle design.

5. Let them all show and tell about what they have drawn.

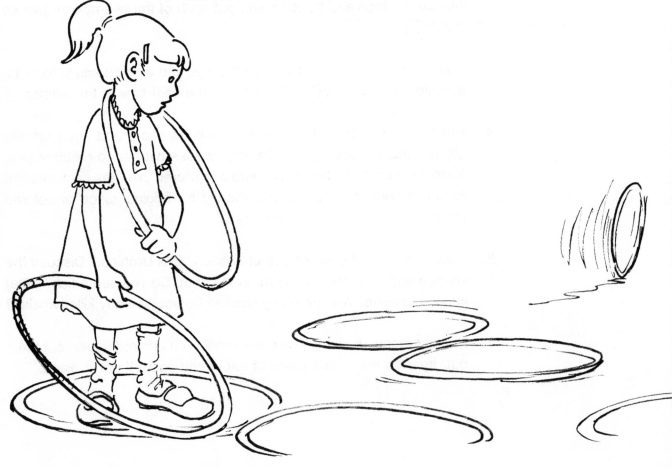

WHO STARTED IT?

OBJECTIVES: To encourage children to begin using their bodies in creative expression.

To increase children's awareness of one another visually.

MATERIALS: Space large enough for children to sit in a circle.

PROCEDURE: 1. Ask one child to leave the room while you select a leader.

2. The leader continually moves all parts of his body while other circle members copy movements.

3. The student who left the room must return to guess who is leading the group.

VARIATION: 1. First child (A) moves some part of his body.

2. Second child (B) repeats A's motion and adds another motion.

3. Third child (C) does A, B, and then adds another, etc. It's fun to see how many times you can go around the circle.

CHANGE THREE

OBJECTIVE: To help develop students' awareness of each other.

MATERIALS: Space large enough for children to sit in a circle.

PROCEDURE:
1. Select two students to stand in the center of the circle.

2. While you count to ten, encourage these students to study each other carefully.

3. Then have students turn back to back and ask them to change three things on themselves (untie shoelace, remove jewelry, unbutton a sleeve, etc.)

4. Again, at the count of ten, have students face each other and discover changes made.

5. **Very young** children will enjoy finding the changes in the concept books entitled *Changes, Changes* by Pat Hutchins (Macmillan, 1971).

11

MIRROR, MIRROR IN THE CIRCLE

OBJECTIVES: To acquaint children with each other.
               To increase visual perceptiveness and concentration.

MATERIALS: Record player and a record album entitled *Blood, Sweat and Tears* by
               Blood, Sweat and Tears.

PROCEDURE: 1. Have children face each other as if looking into a mirror. One child will
                   be the other child's mirror.
                   Have child A make a sad face and child B copy it.
                   Have child B make a happy face and child A copy it.

               2. Encourage child A to move hands, fingers, etc., all very SLOWLY.
                   Play "Theme by Eric Satie" from *Blood, Sweat and Tears* to give slow
                   pace to movement (any slow lyrical music will work).

               3. Child B will reflect child A's movement.

               4. Switch them around so that child B initiates the movement and child A
                   is the mirror.

               5. The students can progress to standing up and mirroring whole body
                   movements if they wish.

"PHIZZOG"

OBJECTIVE: To develop awareness of self.

MATERIALS: Poem entitled "Phizzog" by Carl Sandburg, a baby picture of each student, *Dandylion* by Don Freeman (Macmillan, 1964).

PROCEDURE: 1. Ask students to bring in their own baby pictures.
Collect all pictures.

2. Put them up on the wall to form a Baby Gallery so that no one knows who gave you what picture.

3. Have the class try to guess from the visual characteristics of each baby just who is who.

4. Read the poem entitled "Phizzog" by Carl Sandburg to the class. Discuss it. Does it really matter what you look like on the outside? Younger students will enjoy hearing the story *Dandylion* by Don Freeman showing what can happen if you change your physical appearance.

PHIZZOG
by Carl Sandburg

This face you got,
This here phizzog you carry around
You never picked it out for yourself,
    at all, at all --- did you?
This here phizzog -- somebody handed it to you ---
    am I right?
Somebody said, "Here's yours, now go
    see what you can do with it."
Somebody slipped it to you and it
    was like a package marked:
"No goods exchanged after being
    taken away" ----
This face you got.

STOP! DON'T LOOK! and LISTEN!

OBJECTIVE: To develop auditory awareness by concentrating on sounds around the children.

MATERIALS: Tape recorder, tape, "Procession" from the album *Every Good Boy Deserves Favour* by the Moody Blues.

PROCEDURE:

1. Have children lie on the floor stretched out flat.
2. Ask them to listen to all the sounds inside the room and try to identify them (give them a minute and a half).
3. Ask them to listen to all the sounds outside the room (give them a minute and a half).
4. Then ask children to listen to all the sounds inside their bodies (give them from one to two minutes depending upon attention span).
5. Discuss what everyone heard inside the room (other people breathing, the fan, the lights humming, etc.). Discuss what they heard outside the room (talking, walking, slamming door, traffic in street, etc.). Discuss what each person heard inside his own body (heartbeat, breathing, stomach growling, etc.). Tell the class that by adulthood man's hearing center in the brain is able to distinguish about half a million meaningful sounds.
6. Divide the children into two groups. Allow each group to tape record sounds. Group one will tape inside sounds. Group two will tape outside sounds.
7. Allow groups to listen to each other's tape recording. See how many sounds they can distinguish.
8. You may wish to allow some students to make a tape recording at home. A child might want to record the sounds of one room in his home, for example.
9. Have upper elementary children lie back again and listen to the "Procession" cut on the Moody Blues album. Ask them to listen for the history of the world told in sound.
10. Discuss what they heard. Tell the class that the ear is not only used for hearing but also for helping to keep a sense of balance.

THRUMP-A-DUMP-A-DUMP-A-DUMPA-...

ALL EARS

OBJECTIVES:
To encourage children to begin using their sense of hearing.
To encourage children to begin using their imaginations.
To encourage children to develop listening habits.
To use as a warm-up getting-to-know-you activity.
To offer an instant success experience to children.

MATERIALS:
Noise items such as rubber bands, sandpaper, keys, scissors, castanets, coins, Scotch Tape, bells, beans, marbles, paper clips, bag of potato chips, a zipper and L'eggs eggs or some plastic containers.

PROCEDURE:

1. Ask for one student volunteer to close his eyes.

2. Make sounds with any of the items listed above and ask the student to identify the sound (drop keys, clap hands, stamp foot, shake coins, open and shut scissors, tear open the potato chips, etc.).

3. Once students are accustomed to using their ears, make up sound shakers by placing paper clips in two separate plastic containers such as L'eggs eggs. Put dry beans in two containers, pennies in two containers, marbles in two containers, rice in two containers, gum erasers in two containers, feathers in two containers, hair pins in two containers, etc.

4. Mix the containers up and have the student pick one up at a time, shake it and then try to find the other container that has the same sound by shaking each until the sounds match.

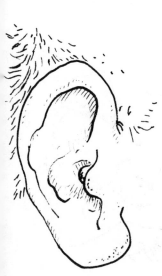

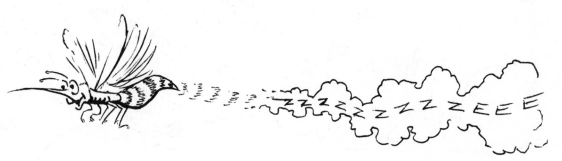

HUMAN VOICE SOUND TRACK

OBJECTIVE: To create sound environments by using only the human voice in order to explore the musical instrument.

MATERIALS: Tape recorder and tape.

PROCEDURE:
1. Group children into 7 or 8 voices for each environment.
2. Assign an environment to each group: a barnyard
   a circus
   a city street
   a baseball game
   a haunted house
3. Get each group talking about the sounds they would hear in their environment. An example:
   a. The barnyard environment would have what sounds? Ducks! Horses! Pigs! Cows! Dogs! What would wake them all up? A Rooster!
   b. The haunted house environment would have what sounds? Squeaking doors! Ghosts! Chains! Thunder! Witch's cackle! Screams! Hooting Owls!
4. Let each group vocally work on its environment by having each member decide which sound to be. Have them decide which sound will start and how the others will be added cumulatively. Have the lightest sound in each case go first and add increasingly heavier sounds to the environment.
5. Give them rehearsal time.
6. Tape each group's sound track one at a time.
7. Replay tapes for the whole class one at a time.

SEEING SOUNDS

OBJECTIVE: To develop auditory and visual relationships.

MATERIALS: Sound-picture sheets, word-sound sheets, pencils.

PROCEDURE:
1. Ask the class to sit in a circle and discuss "sounds" that they like. Have them actually demonstrate what they sound like.

2. Have the class pass a funny sound around the circle with each person adding a sound to the original.

3. Pass out sound-picture sheets and ask the class to write underneath the picture a word-sound which the picture suggests.

4. Pass out the word-sound sheets and ask the class to draw a picture over each one that looks like the word sounds.

5. Have the class share the pictures and sounds with each other.

PLOPSA	THIMM	MIMEONEMEE
GRUFLICK	SOWAMBAW	YAK
SLILLEREL	WAMPET	TICKERTAY
SHOUSH	TOODLELOODLELOO	SHOWMBLURP

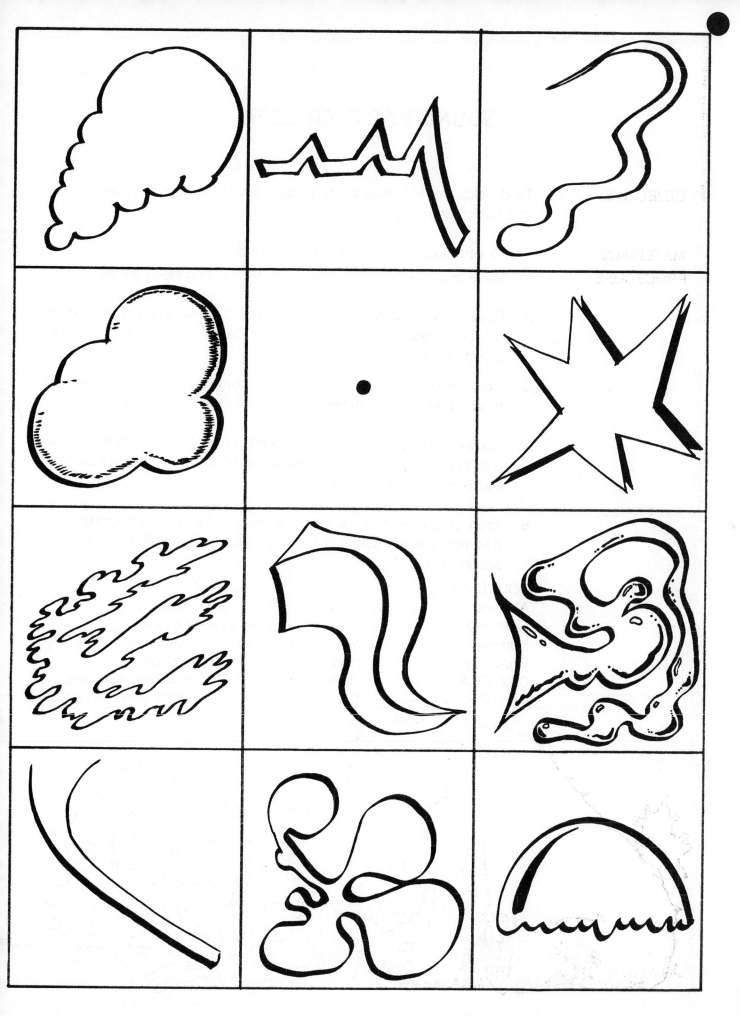

21

SOUND PARTNER SEEK

OBJECTIVE: To develop the selective ability to tune out some sounds while tuning in one particular sound.

MATERIALS: 3 X 5 sound cards for each sound listed below.

PROCEDURE:

1. Make two 3 X 5 sound cards for each sound listed below.

2. Pass out sound cards to all the children. Make sure two of each sound has been assigned. Do not allow students to know who has their duplicate cards.

3. Have children go in all areas of the room, close their eyes and get down on all fours to move around slowly for safety's sake.

4. Children all begin to make **their** sounds at once. (Make sure each student makes the sound that is written on his card, not just say the word that is written on the card.)

5. Each child must find his sound partner by listening and going in the direction that the sound is coming from -- and eventually tagging his sound partner.

SOUND CARDS

Ah-choo	Wheee-----ee!	Buzz
Tick-Tock	Quack Quack (like a duck)	Whistle
Hummm	Moo-oo (like a cow)	Sing ''Happy Birthday''
Growl (grrr-rr-rr)	Heehaw	Hiccup
Click Click	Ha Ha (laughing)	Baa Baa (like a lamb)
Peep Peep	Crying	Bark! Bark! (like a dog)

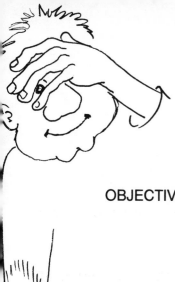

BLIND MAN'S EXPLORATION

OBJECTIVES: To develop sense of touch by concentrating on the textures, shapes, temperatures, and sizes that make up the room and items commonly held.

To encourage children to begin using their sense of touch and imagination.

To use as a getting-to-know-you activity.

To offer instant success experiences to children.

MATERIALS: Blindfold, magic box containing items that could fit easily into a child's hands (vary texture and size). Box can contain anything and everything from paper clips, sandpaper, cotton, pencils, glue, tape, toothpicks, toothpaste, Q-tips, soap, pins, jewelry, staples, plastic bottles, crayons, sponges, hangers, marbles, candy, gum, hair clips, rollers, scissors, mirrors, etc.

PROCEDURE:
1. Ask one child to sit in front of you blindfolded with hands behind his back.
2. Place one item from the box into the child's hands and ask him to identify it. This should be a successful experience. If he cannot identify the item, ask other class members to give hints.
3. When all children have had an opportunity at that exercise, blindfold and ask each child to explore the room with his hands. Start children on all fours close to the floor and have them stay there until they work their way to a wall or a door. (Beware of safety hazards. Electric plugs should have tape over them.)
4. After two to five minutes, depending upon attention span, have them take their blindfolds off and discover where they are. Slow, quiet music in the background will help their concentration.
5. Discuss with the group all the things they felt or thought they felt.

ALL-THUMBS RELAY

OBJECTIVE: To illustrate how much we depend on our fingers with which to touch and manipulate objects.

MATERIALS: Two identical pairs of mittens, a bag of carmels individually wrapped in cellophane.

PROCEDURE:

1. Ask the group to study their hands by having the left hand explore the right hand and vice versa. Are they exactly the same? Check nails, warts, callouses, etc. Have them notice their thumbs. Tell them that the thumb is the most versatile tool for touching and gripping that evolution has ever known. Without the thumb man would not be able to do many of the things that he does in daily living.

2. Divide the class in half and line the two teams up in single file.

3. The first person in each line puts on a pair of mittens and is handed a cellophane-wrapped carmel which must be unwrapped and popped into the mouth.

4. The mittens are handed to the next person in line, relay style. The procedure starts all over again with the unwrapping of the carmel. The team to finish first wins the relay.

24

PENCIL PICK

OBJECTIVE: To develop each child's ability to visualize items by exploring their sizes, shapes, textures, temperatures and weights through touch.

MATERIALS: Thirty pencils in different sizes and shapes and paper sacks.

PROCEDURE:

1.   Divide the class into groups of six to eight.

2.   Give each child a pencil to explore by touching it. Remind the class members to feel its size, shape, texture. Notice its point, its eraser and whether or not it has printing on it. Have each student mark his initial on his pencil somewhere.

3.   Have all children put their pencils into their group's sack.

4.   Shake the sack.

5.   Have each child one at a time reach into the sack and try to find "the" pencil by touching, not looking.

6.   Whether each child is able to find the correct pencil or not, be sure the pencil is put back into the sack before the next child tries.

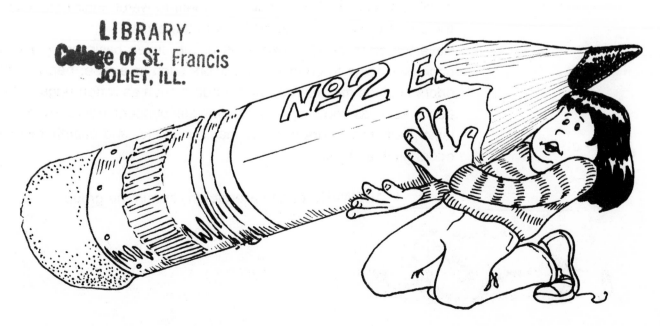

Game 17: Olfactory Awareness

"A ROSE BY ANY OTHER NAME"

SENSORY KIT

OBJECTIVE: To develop the sense of smell as well as visual and gustatory.

MATERIALS: The Sensory Kit: separate jars with lids marked A, B, C, etc.
a. flour   b. salt   c. sugar   d. baking soda   e. peppermint extract
f. lemon extract   g. cinnamon   h. sage   i. licorice   j. mustard
k. peanut butter   l. an orange.

PROCEDURE:

1. Have each child look at the jars with flour, salt, sugar and baking powder and try to tell what they are.
2. Then have them touch each (A-D).
3. Then have them smell each (A-D).
4. Then have them taste each (A-D).
5. Have the children identify peppermint, lemon, cinnamon and sage by smelling each (E-H).
6. Tell the class that the sense of smell is more sensitive than the sense of taste. The taste of most food would be bland if we could not also smell it. Have students plug their noses shut by pinching with their fingers. Next have them try to taste a piece of an orange. Next, have them unplug their noses and taste another piece of orange. Tell them that because the sense of smell cannot be used when they are suffering from a head cold, food does not usually taste right.
7. Have the children guess the identity of licorice and mustard and peanut butter by only **smelling** it (i-k).
8. Tell the class that cave man relied heavily on his nose to tell him where to locate food and where to beware of lurking enemies. The sense of smell is a very primitive sense. Ask them to watch their pets' use of the sense of smell and report back to the class.
9. Have the class bring in examples of the seven basic categories of odor. Ask some to bring in floral odors such as a rose; pepperminty odors such as mint extract; putrid odors such as rotten eggs; musty odors such as roots and moldy leaves; pungent odors such as a lemon; ethereal odors such as magic markers; and camphoraceous odors such as Vicks.

* * * *BEWARE of any allergic children in the group.

26

FOOD, GLORIOUS FOOD

OBJECTIVES: To encourage children to identify tastes and textures through the use of their senses.
To encourage children to begin expressing themselves verbally.
To encourage children to begin experiencing descriptive language.
To encourage children to begin using their imaginations through use of the common medium of food.

MATERIALS: Space large enough for children to move around freely, chocolate chips (sweet), lemons (sour), potato chips (salty), baking chocolate (bitter), peanut butter, ice cubes, spices, fruits, vegetables, crackers, and individual plastic spoons.

PROCEDURE: 1. Tell the class that there are approximately 9,000 taste buds on everyone's tongue. Only in the middle of the tongue are there no taste sensations. The four basic tastes that the tongue distinguishes (with the help of the nose) are sweet, salty, sour and bitter. Have each child taste a piece of a candy bar (sweet), a slice of lemon (sour), a potato chip (salty), and a piece of baking chocolate (bitter).
2. Ask children to blindfold eyes while you place certain foods in the students' mouths, by using plastic spoons, encouraging blindfolded students to identify the food (beware of allergies).
3. Ask children to demonstrate how they might walk across a peanut butter or ice-covered floor. Discuss textures.
4. Ask students to mime eating the food hated the most.
5. Ask students to pretend eating things like spaghetti, lemons, taffy, pickles, marshmallows.
6. Classes will enjoy the book entitled *Eats Poems* by Arnold Adoff (Lothrop, 1979).

MOVEMENT MIME

Introductory Thoughts

Part II

Movement mime has several purposes and can be an asset to all subject areas. It allows students, both participants and audience, to understand the power of communication through use of their bodies. Children can freely express their natural spontaneity by eliminating awkwardness and shyness. Because the imagination is used through the element of play, control of muscles is enhanced painlessly in body movement and mime. Inhibitions are overcome as students are asked to mime people and ideas removed from themselves. Words and props are eliminated, so the imagination is stretched, and students can escape into their fantasy worlds.

Movement and mime have potential in any subject area. How does an egg hatch? How does a machine move? How does old look? How could you be number six?

Creative movement and mime processes are simple to initiate. In order for them to thrive, children must be allowed to function freely in a relaxing, and most importantly, accepting atmosphere. Every attempt a child makes should be highly praised. It is the process, not the result, that counts. This eliminates fear of performance and thus encourages use of the imagination. When initiating any exercise, all children should be involved at once. Everyone does the same thing at the same time at the beginning. After completing several group exercises, the teacher may wish to use volunteers to demonstrate other things.

The exercises in this guide are geared for beginning movement and mime experiences. They can be extended easily, depending upon the group of children.

MOVEMENT WARM UPS

OBJECTIVES: To encourage children to use their bodies through a series of non-threatening exercises.
To encourage children to work together while miming activities familiar to them.

MATERIALS: Any book, space in classroom large enough for children to move around freely.

PROCEDURE: 1.   Divide class into groups of two and ask them to mime opposites like happy-sad, tall-short, fat-skinny, etc.

2.   To allow children to begin moving slightly, ask groups of two or three to mime a favorite sport.

3.   In order to demonstrate the need for total body expression, ask each student to balance a book on his head while following simple directions (kick the right foot, clap, walk three steps, etc.).

4.   Ask children to use total body to mime activities like lifting barbells, partaking in a tug-of-war, pushing a heavy box, catching a soccer ball.

5.   Ask children, one at a time, to mime an everyday activity like brushing teeth, setting table, making bed, drinking orange juice, etc. If you wish, a child may wish to select his own activity and other students can guess the activity or join the task.

6.   Ask children to mime what they will be when they grow up.

7.   Divide children into small groups and assign an environment to each group (bathroom, circus, garage, basement, etc.). Allow groups two minutes to build something (using their whole body) that one might find in that environment (towels, clowns, lawn mower, etc.).

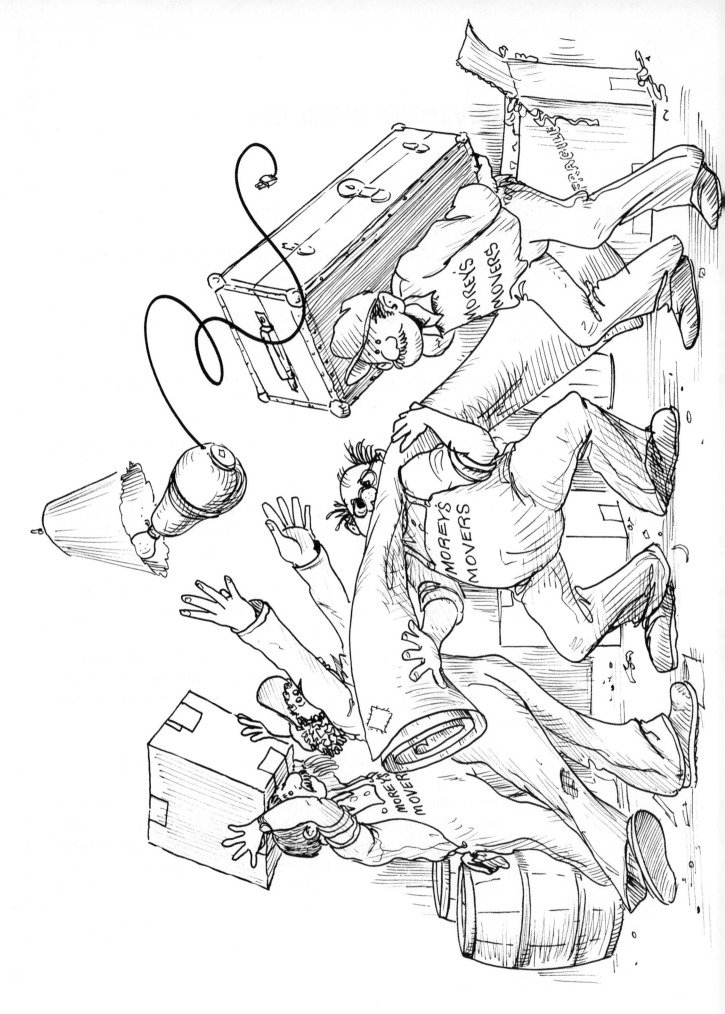

30

ALPHABODIES

OBJECTIVES: To encourage experiences in mime.
               To reinforce the alphabet.

MATERIALS: The book *Alphabeast* (Holt, Rinehart, Winston, 1971) by Dorothy
               Schmiderer and a space large enough for children to move around freely.

PROCEDURE: 1. Share the *Alphabeast* book with the children and encourage them to
                   use their whole bodies (not just hands) while being a letter of the
                   alphabet.

               2. Divide the class into groups. One group of five can be assigned the
                   word "hello." Encourage each child to "be" one of the five letters so
                   that as a group they spell "hello" with their bodies. Another group of
                   five can be given the word "tired." The word "angry" would be an ex-
                   cellent choice for another group of five. Encourage them to let their
                   faces reflect the feeling of the word they have been assigned. Groups
                   of four can work on such words as "love," "hate," "help," "warm,"
                   and "cold."
                   Groups of three can work on such words as "sad," "mad," "old,"
                   "new," and "cry."
                   Words being introduced in the current spelling or reading lesson
                   would also be useful.

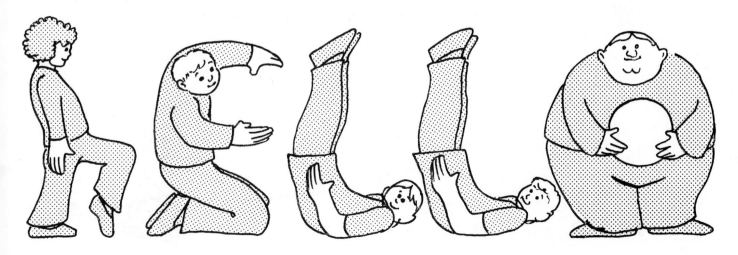

31

ANIMALS

OBJECTIVES: To encourage children to begin using their bodies in creative movement. To make children comfortable with body movement through familiar sources.

MATERIALS: Space large enough for children to move around freely.

PROCEDURE:

1. Ask children to volunteer to be, for example, a rabbit or dog.

2. Once you have a volunteer, ask other children to join in.

3. Slowly build a zoo adding things like snakes, dogs, cats, elephants, lions, etc.

4. Once the "zoo" is built, you may wish to ask several students to mime a family of four walking through the "zoo" reacting to animals. How would different family members react, for example, to a lion or monkey?

5. You may wish to ask children to mime certain animals and ask other children to guess what they are.

6. Ask children for two volunteers, one child to be a puppy and the other to be his master. Tell the master he must train his dog to sit WITHOUT using words and without physical contact. Tell the puppy he is a generally uncooperative character. Allow one minute for presentation.

7. As another creative source, you may wish to refer to *Monday I Was An Alligator* by Susan Pearson (Lippincott, 1979).

SNOWMAN MELT

OBJECTIVES: To relax the entire body to free it from tension.
To increase awareness of shape and form.

MATERIALS: A room.

PROCEDURE:

1. Ask the children if they ever saw a snowman melt in the sun. Discuss the process. Where does the sun first start melting the snowman? How do the parts of the snowman fall off? How does the snowman change shape?

2. Let each child take the position of an upright statue of a snowman.

3. Have children close their eyes and go from a standing snowman to a pool of water by verbalizing these directions slowly:
   a. You are a beautiful, glistening snowman.
   b. The sun shines on your head and you feel the warmth.
   c. The sun gets hotter and the top of your head starts to water and slip. There it goes sliding down to your shoulders.
   d. The sun bathes your shoulders in warmth -- they start to lose their shape and slump over.
   e. Now your body starts to slump over -- your arms and torso crumble.
   f. Your feet and legs begin to shrink. The sun is hot --you fall into your own clump of watery snow on the ground.
   g. The clump slowly dissolves with the heat into a pool of warm water. It is all warm and comfortable and your shape has totally disappeared.

4. You may wish to enhance this activity by discussing the process, and trying it again with the imagery of candles, ice cubes or a dish of ice cream.
   Take children through the oral melting process with each one.

MOP HEAD

OBJECTIVES: To free the entire body and to demonstrate how "good" it feels to move. To make children aware of total body movement.

MATERIALS: Record player and the record *Classical Gas* by Mason Williams.

PROCEDURE:
1. Have the children start by rhythmically shaking just their left hands to the music. The music runs throughout the exercise to keep the shaking motion in a rhythm.

2. Then call out body parts to add to moving parts as the record goes on: right hand, right arm, left arm, torso, shoulders, hips, neck and head and legs.

3. Next ask the children to reverse the process. Call out one body part at a time to put to sleep: legs, hips, torso, neck and head, shoulders, left arm, right arm, right hand, left hand.

POPCORN

OBJECTIVES: To develop the ability to move freely.
              To help children understand form and shape changes.

MATERIALS: Popcorn kernels, popcorn popped, a record player and the album called *Popcorn* by the Hot Buttered.

PROCEDURE:

1. Offer popcorn to the class to eat. Make sure small children chew the popped corn well.

2. Discuss popcorn and kernels with the class. Tell them popcorn is good for their teeth. It makes a good snack because it lacks sugar. Popcorn has a good amount of minerals, niacin and riboflavin. The average person eats about 2.2 pounds of popcorn every year.

3. Have the group touch the kernels of popcorn to feel how hard and smooth-skinned the kernels are.

4. Have the group compare the kernel to the popped corn. It is very fragile and the texture is rough.

5. Ask children to take a spot on the floor and make themselves as small as they can -- like a hard tiny kernel of popcorn.

6. Ask children to squeeze their hands together tightly. Then add feet, legs, arms, stomach, neck and face -- hold them tight and let them go. Explode like a kernel of corn.

7. Divide the children up into groups of 5 or 6. Have each group sit in a circle. Tell them they are kernels in a pan. They will again squeeze, sizzle, explode and bounce around the pan to the music.

8. Get children to tighten their muscles and squeeze as you turn on the heat and the record. Their skin pulls tight, tight, tighter until they explode. Let them bounce in a pan for 1-2 minutes.

9. Read the *Popcorn Dragon* (Morrow, 1953) to the class if you wish to extend the game. *The Popcorn Book* by Tomie de Paola (Holiday House, 1978) is a good source book for the history of popcorn.

THE CRACKED EGG

OBJECTIVE: To develop creative body movement.

MATERIALS: A room and *Horton Hatches the Egg* by Dr. Seuss (Random House, 1940).

PROCEDURE: 1.   Read *Horton Hatches the Egg* by Dr. Seuss.

2.   Talk about how it feels to hatch -- chickens, ducks, and birds. Talk about how it feels to hatch -- new sounds, new sights, new movements.

3.   Have each student find a spot on the floor and curl into the shape of a baby inside an egg.

4.   Ask student to feel the eggshell all around the inside.

5.   Next, have children begin to hit at the shell with wings and feet in order to crack it.

6.   Once students crack the shell they are to climb out as a baby chick, duck, or bird and try to take their first steps in a strange new world.

7.   Do the exercise again and add peeps, quacks, or chirps as the baby breaks out of the egg and tries to walk.

8.   As an extension, refer to *What's Hatching Out of That Egg?* by Patricia Lauber (Crown, 1979).

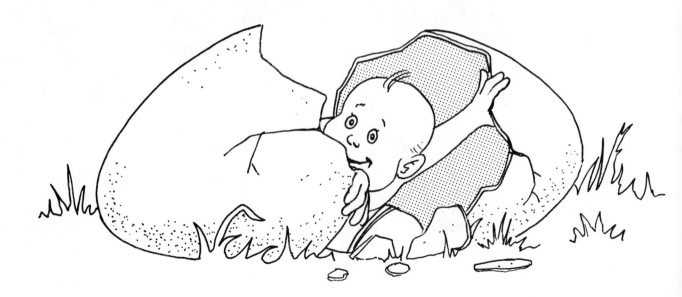

SPROUTS

OBJECTIVES: To develop creative body movement.
To develop an awareness of the beauty in nature --- especially appropriate for spring.
To make students aware of shape and growth.

MATERIALS: Record player, record album entitled *Switched on Bach* by Walter Carlos, pictures of seeds, flowers, trees, gardens, etc.

PROCEDURE:

1. By using pictures lead a discussion with the group about seeds growing and flowering. Have students decide what flowers or trees they would like to be.

2. Have each student get a vivid picture in mind of what his flower or tree looks like when it is full grown by drawing a picture of it. Have him study his flower's or tree's shape. Next, have the student close his eyes and "see" the shape of the tree or flower in his mind.

3. Have students get on the floor and make themselves as small as they can until they feel that they are seeds underground. Tell them they are going to grow from seeds into flowers or trees as the music plays and as you "water" them.

4. Start the "Air on a G String" cut on the *Switched on Bach* album by Walter Carlos and encourage the seeds to poke through the ground and grow and stretch toward the sun and eventually flower.

5. Discuss with each student what flower or tree he was and how each felt.

MERRY MACHINES

OBJECTIVES: To encourage the application of each child's imagination to the ways his body can move.
To promote teamwork.

MATERIALS: Record player and record "Niarobi Trio" from the *Popcorn* album by the Hot Buttered (any music with distinct rhythmic beat throughout will suffice).

PROCEDURE:

1. Show the class the picture of the human machine. Ask them if they can see how the artist has fit the human body into the overall machine.

2. Talk with the group about machinery in general. What machines have they seen? How do they move? Zero in on cogs, wheels, hammers, pistons, etc. How does machine movement compare to human movement?

3. Have the children close their eyes, listen to the record, and visualize a machine.

4. Discuss what each one saw.

5. Put the children in a large circle. Tell them to run to the middle of the circle whenever they get an idea for part of the giant machine the whole class will be making. You may ask one student to volunteer to begin.

6. Put the record on and begin.

7. Try it again. This time encourage the children to add sounds when they add their movements to the machine. Discuss the sounds machines make, for example, bells, whistles, thumps, squeaks, and whirs.

8. As an alternative, children may wish to work in groups of fours building a candy machine with repetitive mechanical movement. One part of the machine must deliver the finished product. At some point in the music, one part of the machine might break down, allowing a repairman to enter the picture.

Human Machine

CHANGES, CHANGES

OBJECTIVE: To develop the ability to start with one movement idea and let it transform into another movement idea.

MATERIALS: A room, record player and record of the sound track to Neil Diamond's *Jonathan Livingston Seagull*.

PROCEDURE:
1. Have children take a place on the floor and react to your directions as they change their bodies from one object into another.
2. Stand up straight. You are a flame on a candle - you flicker your head slightly. Now you are a flag in the breeze - you wave the upper part of your body. Now you are a beautiful big sail on a boat - you wave your whole body.
3. Get down on the floor and stretch out with your stomach on the floor. You are a snake crawling along the grass. Now you are an inchworm crawling and hunching up its back. Now you are a slinky toy crawling and somersaulting.
4. Squat down in a spot on the floor. You are a frog hopping along on two feet. Now you are a rabbit hopping on four feet. Now you are a kangaroo standing upright and hopping on two feet.
5. Curl up like a newborn calf. Then attempt to get up and try out your new shaky legs. Remember you have weak limbs. Next, transform into a loose rag doll walking around. Your legs, arms, neck and head all bob around without any stiffness. Now you transform into a very dizzy person who cannot walk straight.
6. Ask the children to think of flying. Ask each student to choose a bird he would like to be. Discussion should follow.
7. Have each student take a spot on the floor and get into the shape and position of his bird as it is about to take off and fly.
8. Play "Skybird" instrumental cut from the *Jonathan Livingston Seagull* album and direct the birds to take off from their perches and fly. When the music breaks to the second pattern, tell students to transform into kites and keep flying. When the music breaks again, tell them to transform into airplanes and continue to fly until the record is finished.
9. *The Little Red Balloon* by Dela Mari (Barron, 1979) is a beautiful example of a visual idea changing into another visual idea into another and another, etc.

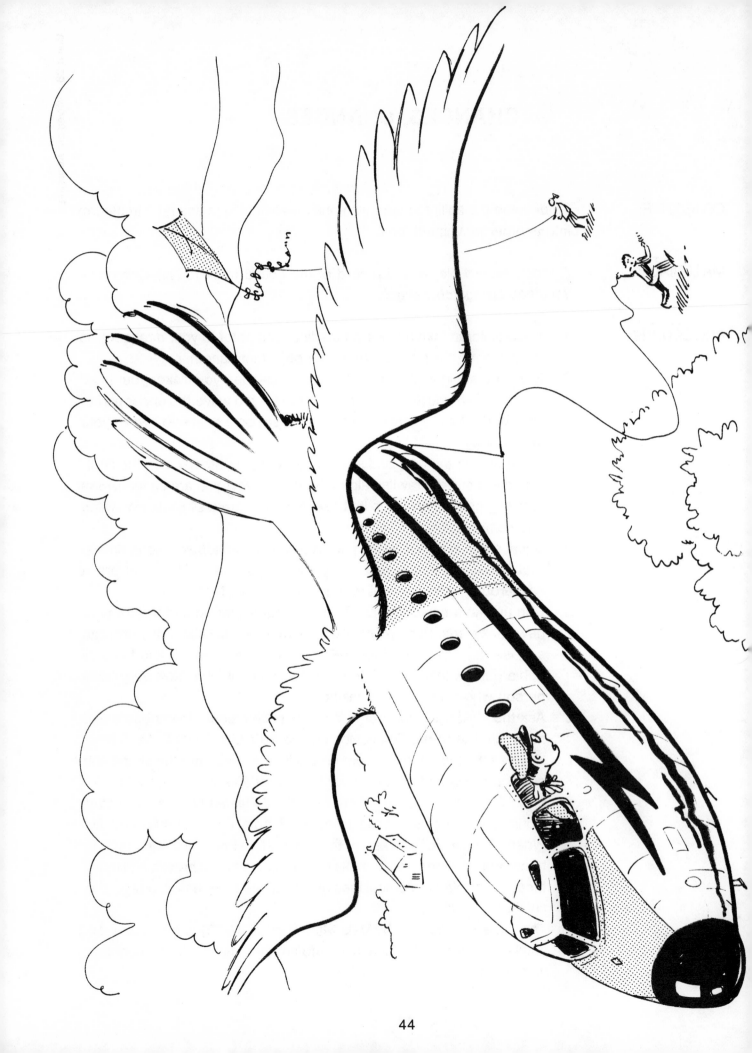

SICK

OBJECTIVES: To encourage children to begin expressing themselves verbally.

To encourage children to begin expressing themselves through body movement.

To allow children to get to know one another.

MATERIALS: "Sick" by Shel Silverstein, pencil, paper, space large enough for children to sit in a circle.

PROCEDURE:
1. Read "Sick" to the children. Discuss the poem. What were Peggy's problems? What caused them? Why do you think she felt that way? Did her mother and father believe her? Have you ever played like you were sick? Why?
2. Ask students to think back to the last time they were *really* sick. How did you feel? What part of your body hurt? Have each student make a sick face as if suffering from a terrible headache.
3. Ask each student to mime (using the face and body) the following "sick" situations:
    a. Show how you feel when you have a toothache.
    b. Let us see how you feel when you have a stomachache.
    c. Show how you would shake if you had chills.
    d. Demonstrate walking with a sprained ankle.
    e. Show how you would climb into bed if you were very weak with the flu.
    f. Mime putting a coat on with a broken arm in a sling.
4. *Ouch: all about cuts and other hurts* by Rita Gelman and Susan Buxbaum (Harcourt, Brace, Jovanovich, 1977) is a wonderful source book for everything from the whys and hows of bumps, burns and black and blue marks to splinters, stitches and scars.

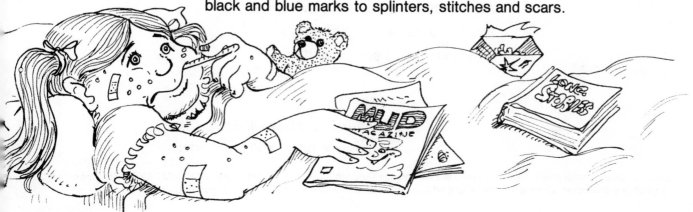

SICK

"I cannot go to school today,"
Said little Peggy Ann McKay.
"I have the measles and the mumps,
A gash, a rash and purple bumps.
My mouth is wet, my throat is dry,
I'm going blind in my right eye.
My tonsils are as big as rocks,
I've counted sixteen chicken pox
And there's one more -- that's seventeen,
And don't you think my face looks green?
My leg is cut, my eyes are blue ---
It might be instamatic flu.
I cough and sneeze and gasp and choke,
I'm sure that my left leg is broke ---
My hip hurts when I move my chin,
My belly button's caving in,
My back is wrenched, my ankle's sprained,
My 'pendix pains each time it rains.
My nose is cold, my toes are numb,
I have a sliver in my thumb.
My neck is stiff, my spine is weak,
I hardly whisper when I speak.
My tongue is filling up my mouth,
I think my hair is falling out.
My elbow's bent, my spine ain't straight,
My temperature is one-o-eight.
My brain is shrunk, I cannot hear,
There is a hole inside my ear.
I have a hangnail, and my heart is - - what?
What's that? What's that you say?
You say today is . . . Saturday?
G'bye, I'm going out to play!"

--Shel Silverstein
Where The Sidewalk Ends
(Harper & Row, 1974)

MONSTER ALIVE!

OBJECTIVE: To develop the ability to create with the body.

MATERIALS: Book called *Movie Monsters* by Thomas Aylesworth (Lippincott, 1975), record player, a record album *2001 Space Odyssey* (sound track).

PROCEDURE:

1. Discuss movie monsters such as Frankenstein, Dracula, Wolf Man, the Mummy, and Hunchback of Notre Dame, by showing pictures from either the book or some other source.

2. Ask children to get up and move like Frankenstein, stiff-legged with arms outstretched. Next, move like the mummy by dragging one leg; move like Dracula by working arms in bat-like fashion; move like the Hunchback all bent over and withered.

3. Have children lie flat on the floor; turn on *2001 Space Odyssey*. Ask each student to get a vivid mental picture of the monster he will become. As the music proceeds, he should come alive and begin to walk around as the monster of his choice.

RED BALLS, BLUE BALLS

OBJECTIVE: To develop the ability to move according to color-moods.

MATERIALS: Record player and the 45 rpm record of "The Entertainer" from *The Sting* and *The Sting* sound track album by Marvin Hamlisch.

PROCEDURE:

1. Discuss with the group the different kinds of balls: tennis balls, footballs, beach balls, Ping-Pong balls, Indian rubber balls, etc.

2. Next, talk with students about how balls move. Stress rolling and bouncing.

3. Have all the children become balls. Encourage them to have a clear picture of what they (as a ball) look like.

4. Start the children in different areas of the room. Have them get down into the round shapes of their balls and start rolling.

5. Next, have them explore rolling and bouncing (at all times each must be a particular kind of ball).

6. During rest period ask the group what color they would call happy? What color is sad? (Usually red stands for happy and blue for sad.)

7. Ask students to choose a color for their ball and roll and bounce in a happy mood or a sad mood according to the color they select. Adjust the 45 rpm record of "The Entertainer" to 33⅓ rpm in order to slow the speed for the sad balls. Adjust the 33⅓ rpm cut of "The Entertainer" from *The Sting* album to 45 rpm for the happy balls.

8. Discuss with the group the balls, colors and moods that they explored.

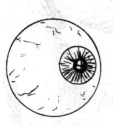    

HAUNTED HOUSE

OBJECTIVE: Psycho-motor development

MATERIALS: Record player, recording of "In The Hall of the Mountain King" from *Peer Gynt* by Grieg, aluminum foil, ribbons, and "The Haunted House" by Jack Prelutsky.

PROCEDURE:

1. Read "The Haunted House" poem while focusing on the picture with the class.

2. Ask children what they think they would find in a haunted house.... ghosts!

3. Have children close their eyes and listen to "In The Hall of the Mountain King" by Grieg *(Peer Gynt)* and see things that go bump in the night dancing around.

4. Discuss what they all saw. Talk about good spirits versus evil spirits or ghosts versus people.

5. Divide the group up between those who want to be good spirits and those who want to be evil spirits. Good spirits will tie ribbons to their wrists and evil spirits will wrap their fingertips in aluminum foil to make long scary nails.

6. Have the good spirits find a spot on the floor and pretend to fall asleep. The evil spirits will enter as the music starts and sneak around the sleeping spirits. As the music develops, the good spirits wake up and there is a dance-chase until all the good spirits are captured and the record is completed.

THE HAUNTED HOUSE

On a hilltop bleak and bare
looms the castle of despair,
only phantoms linger there
within its dismal walls.
Through the dark they're creeping, crawling,
frenzied furies battling, brawling,
sprawling, calling, caterwauling
through the dusky halls.

Filmy visions, ever flocking,
dart through chambers, crudely mocking,
rudely rapping, tapping, knocking
on the crumbling doors.
Tortured spirits whine and wail,
they grope and grasp, they wildly flail,
their hollow voices rasp and rail
beneath the moldering floors.

by Jack Prelutsky

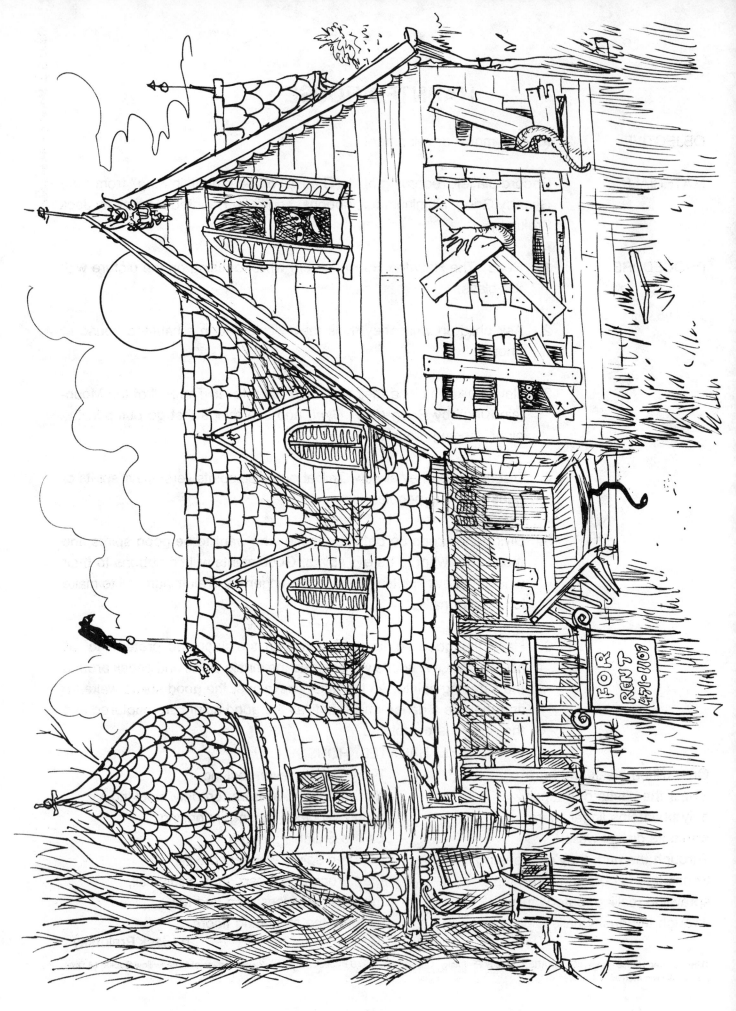

GOOEY, GLUEPY GARBAGE

OBECTIVE: To encourage the child's imagination as applied to body movement.

MATERIALS: "Sarah Cynthia Sylvia Stout," a poem by Shel Silverstein.

PROCEDURE:

1. Set the environment by asking the students if they have to do any chores around the house that they do not like to do.

2. Discussion should follow.

3. Tell them that you have a poem about a little girl called "Sarah Cynthia Sylvia Stout" who had to do something she hated around the house. Read the poem about the girl who would not take the garbage out.

4. Discuss the poem. Get children's reactions. Ask them to get into groups of 2 or 3 and select a piece of garbage they would collectively like to be. The garbage does not have to have been mentioned in the poem.
   a. bacon frying
   b. ice-cream cone melting
   c. bubble gum being chewed
   d. eggs scrambling
   e. milk curdling
   f. a banana being peeled

5. Go from group to group encouraging them and helping them with their imaginative idea.

6. After ten minutes or so ask each group one at a time to show their garbage while the rest of the class guess what it is.

SARAH CYNTHIA SYLVIA STOUT

Sarah Cynthia Sylvia Stout

Would not take the garbage out!

She'd boil the water

and open the cans

and scrub the pots

and scour the pans

and grate the cheese

and shell the peas

and mash the yams

and spice the hams,

and make the jams.

But though her daddy

would scream and shout,

she would not take the garbage out

And so it piled up to the ceilings;

Coffee grounds, potato peelings,

molding bread and withered greens,

olive pits and soggy beans,

cracker boxes, chicken bones,

clamshells, eggshells, stale scones,

sour milk and mushy plums,

crumbly cake and cookie crumbs.

At last the garbage piled so high

that finally it reached the sky.

And none of her friends would come to play.

And all the neighbours moved away.

And finally Sarah Cynthia Stout

said, "I'll take the garbage out!"

But then, of course, it was too late.

The garbage reached beyond the state,

from Memphis to the Golden Gate.

And Sarah met an awful fate,

which I cannot right now relate

because the hour is much too late.

But, children, think of Sarah Stout

and always take the garbage out!

by Shel Silverstein

MISS CHOCOLATE AND MR. LEMON

OBJECTIVE: To develop the imaginative use of the body with which to communicate.

MATERIALS: Pieces of cheese, peanut butter and spoons, cut lemons, marshmallows, pieces of sweet chocolate, gingersnaps, bananas, dill pickles and baking chocolate.

PROCEDURE:

1. Have children come up and choose whatever food they want.

2. Ask them to find a place in the room; sit down and put the food in their mouths and notice **how** the food **moves** in their mouths.

3. Concentrate on this movement and let this sticky, puckery, etc., movement invade the rest of the body.

4. Tell the students to stand up and move across the room like the food moves in their mouths --- smoothly, stickily, jerkily, etc.

5. Develop a character from this movement -- a lemony-sour person, a chocolate-sweet person, a gingersnappy-abrupt person, etc.

6. Ask for volunteers to move across the floor like their food characters while the rest of the class guess from what food each character evolved.

TOYS ALIVE!

OBJECTIVE: To develop imaginative use of the body.

MATERIALS: *Nutcracker Suite* by Tchaikovsky, record player, a picture of a viaduct and a pile of toys brought from home by the children.

PROCEDURE:

1. Show children a picture of a viaduct. Ask them if this kind of structure can move. Discuss the shape of the viaduct and the possibility of its legs coming to life. Have students stand up and visualize themselves as cement viaducts. Ask them to stiffen their arms out straight, stiffen their legs, and stiffen their backbones and necks. Next, encourage children to walk around the room as rigidly structured viaducts.

2. Continue the class with a discussion of the toys the students have at home or have had in the past.

3. Continue the discussion. Discuss how certain toys move --- a jack-in-the-box pops up on a spring, a robot walks stiff-legged with very jerky head movements, rag dolls have legs like spaghetti all weak and limp, wind-up cars zing along, pogo sticks bounce.

4. Have each child choose a toy from the pile and explore how it moves.

5. Put "Dance of the Sugar Plum Fairy" on from *Nutcracker Suite* by Tchaikovsky and have a parade of toys around the room.

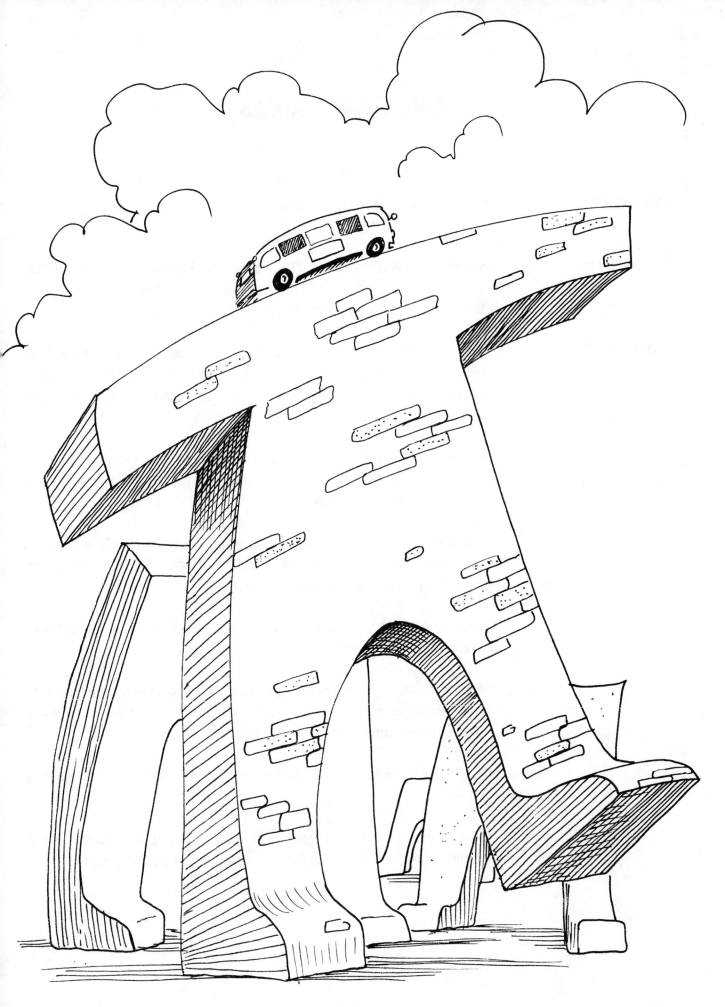

BIKES AND TRIKES

OBJECTIVES: To develop the ability to move the body creatively.
To develop teamwork.

MATERIALS: Record player, record entitled *The Paper Bag Players* by the Paper Bag Players, or any lively music, and the book entitled *The Bike Lesson* by Jan and Stan Berenstain (Random House, 1964).

PROCEDURE:

1. Teachers of lower grades should begin this game by reading *The Bike Lesson* to the class. Follow with a discussion of rules for bike safety. Teachers of higher elementary grades may wish to begin the game with step 2.

2. Show children the bike montage. Discuss various types of bikes -- bicycles, tricycles, unicycles, bicycles built for two, weight reduction bikes, etc. Be sure to ask them to describe their bikes.

3. Have students close their eyes and visualize a scene with a bike in it while you play "Bicycle Race" from the Paper Bag Players' album (only lively music will work as a substitute).

4. Discuss the mental picture that each student saw. What particular type of bike was seen?

5. Put the class in groups of five and ask each group to form a bike with their bodies and have the bike move. Some students will be wheels, others riders, others handlebars, etc.

6. Put "Bicycle Race" on and have each group demonstrate how its bike moves.

7. A bicycle race among the groups is a fine follow up **if** there is room. A starting line could be established along with rules and judges.

RAIN, RAIN GO AWAY

OBJECTIVES: To introduce three types of cloud formations -- cirrus, cumulus and stratus.

To encourage creative body movement.

MATERIALS: *The Cloud Book* by Tomie de Paola (Holiday House, 1975), a thunder sheet (a piece of sheet metal).

PROCEDURE:

1. Introduce the topic of clouds by letting the class view the clouds outside and asking children what they see (shapes, animals, faces).
2. Read *The Cloud Book* to the class.
3. Discuss three types of cloud formations and review their shapes and functions. (If possible go outside and view the clouds. Try to label them. See pictures in the clouds, also.)
4. Ask the whole class to become cirrus clouds. Remind them that cirrus clouds are very high in the sky. Move tall. Glide.
5. Ask the whole class to become cumulus clouds. Shape the body like marshmallow puffs. Move close to the ground. Keep changing the billowy shape.
6. Next, ask everyone to try on the shape of stratus clouds. Remember they are very long strips or ribbons of gray. Stretch the body.
7. Review the characteristics of cumulonimbus clouds. They are a group of many cumulus clouds, piled mountain high which carry rain for thunderstorms.
8. Form groups of six or seven students each and have them start in a body pile and slowly grow to form a group cumulonimbus cloud. Encourage the composite cloud to move around the room.
9. Enact a summer thunderstorm. Cast thunderbolts, lightning, cirrus clouds, cumulus clouds and a group cumulonimbus cloud. Begin with a beautiful calm sky full of cirrus clouds floating all around. Have cumulus clouds move in and group together to form a cumulonimbus cloud. Next, encourage the lightning to zigzag dramatically through the clouds, stirring them up as the storm becomes violent. Shake the thunder sheet. Turn lights on and off until the storm peaks and begins to roll away.

"SAID THE SPIDER TO THE FLY"

OBJECTIVES: To develop creative body movement.

To develop teamwork.

MATERIALS: Nursery rhyme "Said the Spider to the Fly," record player, record album entitled *Snowflakes Are Dancing* by Tomita.

PROCEDURE:

1. Begin by discussing how the spider spins her web in order to catch food. Spiders make silk from liquid inside their bodies; the silk comes out of the body through the spinneret. The spider is not an insect because it has eight legs, not six. The spider is also without wings and antennae. It has only two body divisions -- head and abdomen. Flies and other insects are caught in the web when they touch the sticky substance. Show students the picture of web patterns.

2. Read the nursery rhyme "Said the Spider to the Fly" to the class.

3. Have students close their eyes and listen to the *Snowflakes Are Dancing* album and see if they can visualize the spider spinning her web, the fly fluttering around it, getting caught, then getting caught more and more as she tries to get free, the reappearance of the spider and finally the killing of the fly by the spider.

4. Cast the part of the spider and the part of the fly.

5. Cast 6-8 students as the web and give them time to work out their design with the spider. (They must be able to hold on to the fly when she comes too near.)

6. Start the music and let the scene develop by using creative movement.

7. Recast in order to let others participate.

8. The book *Aranea: a story about a Spider* by Jenny Wagner (Bradbury, 1975) is a fine story about how hard a spider works to construct a web.

Said the Spider to the Fly

"Will you walk into my parlor?" said the spider to the fly---
"Tis the prettiest little parlor that ever you did spy.
The way into my parlor is up a winding stair;
And I have many curious things to show you when you're there."
"Oh, no, no," said the little fly; "to ask me is in vain;
For who goes up your winding stair can ne'er come down again."

"I'm sure you must be weary, dear, with soaring up so high;
Will you not rest upon my little bed?" said the spider to the fly.
And if you like to rest awhile, I'll snugly tuck you in!"
"Oh, no, no," said the little fly; "for I've often heard it said,
They never, never wake again, who sleep upon your bed!"

Said the cunning spider to the fly---
"Dear friend, what can I do
To prove the warm affection I've always felt for you?"
"I thank you, gentle sir," she said, "for what you're pleased to say,
And bidding you good-morning now, I'll call another day."
The spider turned him round about, and went into his den,
For well he knew the silly fly would soon come back again;
So he wove a subtle web in a little corner sly,
And set his table ready, to dine upon the fly.
Then he came out to his door again, and merrily did sing---
"Come hither, hither, pretty fly, with the pearl and silver wing;
Your robes are green and purple -- there's a crest upon your head!
Your eyes are like the diamond bright but mine are dull as lead!"

Alas! alas! how very soon this silly little fly,
Hearing his wily, flattering words, came slowly flitting by.
With buzzing wings she hung aloft, then near and nearer drew;
Thinking only of her brilliant eyes, her green and purple hue---
Thinking only of her crested head--poor foolish thing! At last,
Up jumped the cunning spider, and firmly held her fast!
He dragged her up his winding stair, into his dismal den,
Within his little parlor -- but she ne'er came out again!

And now, dear little children, who may this story read,
To idle, silly, flattering words, I pray you ne'er give heed;
Unto an evil counselor close heart, and ear and eye,
And take a lesson from this tale of the Spider and the Fly.

ART AWARENESS
Introductory Thoughts
Part III

Line, shape, space and color surround us every day and make up the images that are our environment. But extraordinary arrangements of these elements are not everyday occurrences. Awareness of and appreciation for these events on canvas as created by civilizations' visual artists should be developed in all children at an early age. Consequently, a number of fine art prints are identified here as both useful and appropriate to certain games.

Each fine art print suggested can be used as either a stimulant for thought and conversation or a cultural supplement to a game. Most of the prints are readily available from resource centers and/or the library. Furthermore, it is not necessary to have an in-depth knowledge of "art" in order to creatively use the following masterpieces. All that is needed is the desire to participate in the joy of the aesthetic experience.

Diego Rivera, Mexican muralist, set off an angry controversy when he painted *Man and Machinery* on the walls of the Detroit Institute of Arts in 1932. Since big money paid for the mural, it was hoped that the working man's conditions would be glorified. However, as the picture illustrates, the working conditions were not positively portrayed. Rivera was a proletarian and had always championed the plight of the peasant and the worker. As supported by *Man and Machinery,* Rivera was a master at filling huge spaces. This picture can be effectively used in conjunction with the "Live Photography - Tableau" game.

Vincent Van Gogh was another artist who was obsessed with painting. He was always compelled to finish a painting at one sitting. *The Artist's Bedroom at Arles* shows his dominant use of bright reds and yellows. In fact, Van Gogh painted his entire house on the outside in yellow so that it would be a house of light for everyone. He desperately needed companionship but his temper and emotionality drove people away from him. Born in 1853, the Dutch artist had to deal with the fact that he was a second Vincent Van Gogh --- a year prior, a son, also named Vincent, was born to his parents. He died right after birth. His father, a preacher, had the first Vincent's tombstone in plain view for all to see as they entered the church. Whether this bothered the second Vincent or not, the fact remains that Van Gogh struggled for sanity off and on throughout his life. In fact, he died in 1890 at the early age of thirty-seven from a self-inflicted gunshot wound. This picture is a wonderful example for the "Go To Your Room" game.

Spanish artist El Greco was born Domenicos Theolocopoulos on the Greek island of Crete in 1548. He adopted the city of Toledo, Spain, as his second home. In fact, his picture entitled *View of Toledo* is the first pure landscape in Spanish art. Interesting to note, this strong turbulent picture was made more dramatic by the artist's relocation of the church from the center of town to hillside. El Greco, having dedicated most of his talent to the church, died in 1614. This painting can be effectively used with the "Haunted House" game.

Picasso had his first exhibition at the age of sixteen. Although he worked in a number of styles, the Spanish artist evolved Cubism in 1881. His father, an art teacher, encouraged him at the age of ten to draw. So prolific at his art and craft, Picasso sometimes painted up to three pictures a day! Possibly the most well-known painter in the world, Picasso died in 1973 at the age of ninety-two. His *Three Musicians* is a fascinating creation in geometric shapes. It would be a most useful stimulus for the "Shape Completion" game.

At the age of eighty Anna Mary Robertson Moses began to seriously paint. In fact, Grandma Moses, as she came to be known, completed twenty-five paintings after her 100th birthday! Born in 1860, Grandma Moses spent the first ten years of her life on a farm. At twelve years of age she left home as a hired girl. After a full life spent raising ten of her own children, Grandma Moses put her primitive style on canvas. She captured the charm of American country life. She was 101 years old at the time of her death in 1961. *A Tramp On Christmas Day* is full of details that lead to both facts and assumptions. This picture is an effective source for the "Fact vs. Fancy" game.

The Peaceable Kingdom was painted 100 times by American artist Edward Hicks! The 100 versions have much in common with one another. A self-taught preacher of the Quaker faith, Hicks was most obsessed with the eleventh chapter of the Book of Isaiah: "The wolf shall dwell with the lamb, and the leopard shall lie down with the kid, the calf and the young lion together; and a little child shall lead them." This painting is useful in conjunction with the "Pieced Peace" game.

Three Women was painted in 1921 by the French artist Fernand Leger. He was greatly criticized for dehumanizing the human body. Another point of view, however, would be to see the painting in praise of how beautifully the human body can function. One of the leading artists in the Cubist style, Leger managed to incorporate the three women, their breakfast table and their cat totally in the geometric environment. This picture is a wonderful visual stimulus for the "Merry Machines" game.

Graphic master M. C. Escher felt that he had more in common with mathematicians than artists. His precision as it relates to filling his space is almost hypnotic to the eye of the beholder. The fascinating woodcut, *Sky and Water II* is a good example of visual transformation. Born in Holland in 1898, Escher was both a superb craftsman and imaginative artist. He died in 1972. This is an effective print to use in connection with the "Changes, Changes" game.

WHO SAID MICHELANGELO?

OBJECTIVES: To help children communicate without words.

To encourage children to work together.

MATERIALS: Two sheets of paper, two crayons, magic box full of such articles as listed in Game #14.

PROCEDURE:
1. Divide children into two teams.
2. Each team member then takes a number.
3. The teacher calls out a number. The student with that number from each team leaves the room with the teacher.
4. The teacher shows the two students one item from the magic box.
5. The students return to respective teams, NOT TALKING. They immediately draw a picture of the item just displayed.
6. Other team members must guess the item.
7. The team that discovers the identity of the item first gets the point. Teacher calls another number and one student from each team looks at another item from the magic box.
8. The procedure goes on until all members of each team have seen an object and attempted to draw it.
9. The team with most points is the winner.

"JABBERWOCKY"

OBJECTIVES:	To stimulate the imagination by the use of poetic imagery.
	To develop teamwork in order to produce group art.
MATERIALS:	The poem, "Jabberwocky" by Lewis Carroll, butcher paper, tape and felt tipped markers.
PROCEDURE:	1. Read the poem "Jabberwocky" to the class.

2. Discuss the Jabberwock in particular with the class. What do you think it looks like? Would it have hair? Is it short? Does it have more than two eyes?

3. Tape strips of butcher paper on the wall so that you have a huge square of paper. Tell the students that they are going to make a **group** picture of what the Jabberwock could look like.

4. First ask if anyone has an idea of how the head would be shaped. Invite one of the students who has an idea to come up to the paper and draw the head. Next, ask someone else to add the hair. Then someone else can add the face. In this way each member of the entire class will add an element to the physical picture of the Jabberwock by using the imagination.

5. If the class is still excited about what it has created, you can ask students to draw a composite picture of what the Jabberwock's family would look like --- further stimulating the students' imaginations.

JABBERWOCKY

"Twas brillig, and the slithy toves
    Did gyre and gimble in the wabe;
All mimsy were the borogoves,
    And the mome raths outgrabe.

"Beware the Jabberwock, my son!
    The jaws that bite, the claws that catch!
Beware the Jubjub bird, and shun
    The frumious Bandersnatch!"

He took his vorpal sword in hand:
    Long time the manxome for he sought---
So rested he by the Tumtum tree,
    And stood awhile in thought.

And as in uffish thought he stood.
    The Jabberwock, with eyes of flame,
Came whiffling through the tulgey wood.
    And burbled as it came!

One, two! One, two! and through and through
    The vorpal blade went snicker-snack!
He left it dead, and with its head
    He went galumphing back.

"And hast thou slain the Jabberwock?
    Come to my arms, my beamish boy!
O frabjous day! Callooh! Callay!"
    He chortled in his joy.

"Twas brillig, and the slithy toves
    Did gyre and gimble in the wabe:
All mimsy were the borogoves,
    And the mome raths outgrabe.

by Lewis Carroll

ME

OBJECTIVE: To encourage each student to become self-aware.

MATERIALS: Rolls of butcher paper and assorted felt tipped markers.

PROCEDURE:

1. Tell the class they are going to draw a self-portrait----but it will not be an ordinary self-portrait.

2. Ask students in the group the following questions: What food do you like? What television shows do you like? What seasons are your least favorite? What are your best-liked hobbies? What geographic area do you enjoy? What relatives...What customs, etc.? Cover all areas of each individual's likes and dislikes.

3. Roll out the butcher paper and ask the class to work in pairs. Each pair has 12 feet of paper.

4. Ask student A to lie down on the butcher paper while student B makes a complete outline of his partner's body with a felt tipped marker.

5. Student B then lies down as student A makes an outline of that body.

6. Each student cuts out the body silhouette and tapes it to the wall.

7. Students are now asked to start filling in their own body outlines with all the things that make up what is liked and disliked -- draw foods that are liked, people that are liked, weather, books, hobbies, habits, styles, music, celebrities, colors, and countries that are liked. Draw the likes on the left hand side of the body outline and the dislikes on the right-hand side.

8. Share each picture in the "Me Gallery" by walking from one to the other. Each student will comment, explain and interpret his own picture as the group views it.

GO TO YOUR ROOM

OBJECTIVE: To visually awaken each student to the detailed aspects of an environment in which he spends a great deal of time - his bedroom.

MATERIALS: Accompanying picture entitled, "Bedroom at Our House," drawing paper and felt tipped pens.

PROCEDURE:

1. Show the class the picture entitled "Bedroom at Our House." Discuss the details in the room: pictures on the wall, living things, mechanical toys, clothing and the tape used to hang the pictures. Does this picture tell you anything about the child's interests? How many items can you identify in the closet? In what ways does this picture remind you of your own bedroom?

2. Ask each student to close his eyes and visualize his own bedroom. What color is it painted? Are there any pictures on the wall? Are there any stuffed animals on the bed? Is there any evidence of hobbies in the room?

3. Pass out drawing paper and felt tipped markers to each student. Ask each to sketch a picture of his bedroom and color it.

4. Have students take their drawings home and compare them to what they see. Ask them to examine their rooms---looking for cracks, colors, patterns, and things that they were never aware of before. Direct each to draw another picture of his room while he is studying it.

5. Next day, have all the students bring their first and second pictures back in order to share with the entire class. What did they find out about their bedrooms? How do the first (recall drawing) and the second drawings compare?

Bedroom at Our House

PIECED PEACE

OBJECTIVES: To develop visual awareness.

To develop an ability to create a certain feeling visually by means of a collage.

MATERIALS: An assortment of pictorial magazines, scissors, paste, Bristol boards, and the accompanying picture entitled "Peaceable Jungle."

PROCEDURE:

1. Show "Peaceable Jungle" to the class. Discuss the following questions: How does it make you feel? What titles can you think of for it? Is it peaceful? How do you know? What makes the animals look peaceful? Have you seen anything peaceful today? What?

2. Ask groups of students to construct a tableau of "Peaceable Jungle" with their own bodies. Let them cast themselves as the lion, etc., (notice the eyes).

3. Pass out magazines, scissors, paste and Bristol board and ask each student to create a collage on the theme of peace by cutting pictures, words, symbols, moods, situations and expressions of peace out of the magazines. Arrange and paste them on the Bristol board.

4. Examine each student's conception of "peace" by sharing each collage.

Peaceable Jungle

DRAW ME A POEM

OBJECTIVE: To introduce the class to concrete poetry through visual art.

MATERIALS: Large white drawing paper, lead pencils, colored pencils, erasers and the poems entitled, "Free Flight" and "Slow Poke."

PROCEDURE:

1. Read the poem "Slow Poke" to the class. Hand out copies. Discuss the visual impact of the poem when you see it on the printed page. Note that the author has created the shape of his subject by **filling** the shape in with words.

2. Read the poem "Free Flight" to the class. Hand out copies. Discuss the visual impact of the poem when you see it on the printed page. Note that the author has created the shape of his subject by outlining the shape with words.

3. Ask students to close their eyes and think about spring. What do you see? Are there any flowers? Birds? Trees? Sun? Are there any animals scurrying around? Balloons? Umbrellas?

4. Choose one of your spring images and put your body into its shape. Close your eyes. Start to move as the image you choose would move. Explore the shape, movement and feeling.

5. Pass out the large drawing sheets and pencils. Ask each student to draw a pencil outline of the spring image selected.

6. Then ask each student to write a description of his image with colored pencils inside the pencil outline or write a description of the image on the pencil outline itself. How did you feel when you were the image? What sights, sounds, feelings, smells, and movements are tied up with the image?

7. When the students have completed their descriptions by either filling in the pencil drawings or placing the words on the pencil outline, have them erase the pencil outlines. They will be left with concrete poems.

Slow Poke

Free Flight

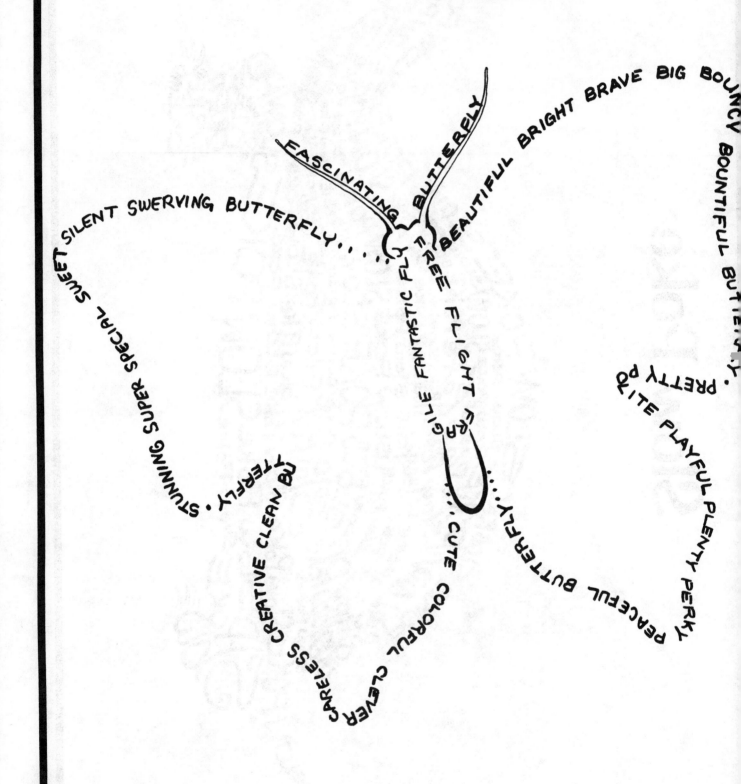

CURVES AHEAD!

OBJECTIVES: To introduce the concept of the simple closed curve.
To explore the use of slides as a vehicle for design.

MATERIALS: Large sheets of drawing paper, felt tipped markers, double glass slide binders, a set of overhead projection pens, slide projector, screen, record player and the record "The Windmills of Your Mind" by Ferrante and Teicher.

PROCEDURE:

1. Give each child a piece of paper and a marker. Ask each to draw a rainbow. When all are finished, tell them that they have just drawn a curve. Ask them to draw other curves such as bridges, arches and the digit 3.

2. Next, ask the class to draw a zero. Tell students they have just drawn a simple closed curve. Ask them if they can see the difference between curves and simple closed curves. Draw some more simple closed curves --- heart shapes, the sun and the printed upper-case letter D.

3. Ask the students to draw the digit 8. Tell them this is not a simple closed curve because the curve crosses itself. Have them draw other examples of closed curves that are not simple closed curves --- a bow and a pretzel.

4. Divide the class into three groups. Each member of group #1 will draw designs made up of curves on the glass slides given to them. Each member of group #2 will draw designs made up of simple closed curves on the glass slides given to them. And each member of group #3 will draw designs made up of closed curves that cross themselves. Have students draw to the music of "The Windmills of Your Mind."

5. Put on a slide show of all the designs with the record "The Windmills of Your Mind" as accompaniment.

"PANDORA'S BOX"

OBJECTIVE: To develop each child's ability to transfer how an emotion feels to how the same emotion would visually look.

MATERIALS: "Pandora's Box," drawing board, felt tipped markers, flat ruler-like sticks, glue and the picture entitled "Spirits."

PROCEDURE: 1. Read "Pandora's Box" to the class.

2. Ask the group to discuss all the grief-like spirits that could have escaped from Pandora's Box. Concentrate on jealousy, pain, grief, hate, fright, anger and death.

3. Explore each visually. How would you draw anger? What color would you color jealousy or death? In what shape would pain hold his mouth? Show the students the accompanying picture entitled "Spirits." Have the children identify the emotions.

4. Ask each student to select one of the terrible spirits and make a mask that stands for that spirit. Pass out markers, drawing boards and flat rulers. Masks are very easy to construct. Mask bases can be made from cardboard with stick or ruler attached. Have on hand a box full of scrap materials, construction paper, buttons, ribbons, and other odds and ends. Encourage students to be creative (it is not necessary to "copy" the pictured masks).

5. Older children may enjoy exploring each emotion in more depth by coming to the front of the class with their masks over their faces and responding to questions thrown out by the rest of the class. For instance, "jealousy" could be asked what it is jealous of and if it has ever tried to control jealousy. Fear could be asked what makes everyone fearful. Each student should be encouraged to answer in character.

79

NOAH'S ARK

OBJECTIVES: To develop the ability of each student to use commonly found materials.

To creatively construct an environment.

To develop teamwork.

MATERIALS: *Captain Noah and His Floating Zoo* by Michael Flanders (Bobbs-Merrill, 1972), a junk pile of art supplies and the accompanying picture entitled "Noah Floats."

PROCEDURE:

1. Show the accompanying picture, "Noah Floats," to the class. Ask students what animals they can identify. Are the animals happy? How many animals are there in the picture? What animals would you invite aboard an ark if you were Noah **today**?

2. Read *Captain Noah and His Floating Zoo* by Michael Flanders to the class.

3. Review with the class the characteristics of the ark. Then, ask them how they could embellish the ark; think of flags, signs, colors, and banners.

4. Divide the class in half and have each team build an ark structure out of "found" materials - boxes, boards, wastepaper baskets, ladders, cardboard, rocks, tin cans, etc. Have a junk pile available of tape, colored paper, pens, rags, etc.

5. When the arks have been created take a tour through each with a designated Noah from each team acting as tour guide.

6. Take a snapshot of each ark before it is taken apart. Display the photographs.

7. Very young students may enjoy the book entitled *Mr. and Mrs. Noah* by Lois Lenski (Crowell, 1948).

Noah Floats

JUNGLE JOKES

OBJECTIVES: To develop a sense of humor through the technique of incongruity.

To develop team body work.

MATERIALS: Large drawing paper, felt tipped markers, record player and record album, *Electronic Evolution* by Hayman and Sear (optional) and accompanying picture entitled "Jungle Mistake."

PROCEDURE:

1. Discuss with the group the idea of putting two things together in order to make a third thing. For example, if we put a pig and a cat together, we might get a "pigat." Ask students to think of what would happen if they put two different animals together. What kind of crazy animal would they get?

2. Put the group in pairs and give them one sheet of paper between them plus felt tipped markers. Have students draw an imaginary animal by putting two animals together. Put Melody #2 on the record player at 45 rpm for crazy jungle mood.

3. When students have finished their drawing ask them to give it a name. Then tape it up on the wall.

4. When all new animals are on the wall ask each inventor-pair to tell the the rest of the group what it is, what it eats, where it lives and **how it moves**. (A half rabbit and half bird would probably have hopping feet and flopping wings.)

5. Next, ask each pair to find a place on the floor and work out the movement of the animal they have invented. Move across the floor as the animal itself.

6. Put Melody #2 on and have a "Jungle Joke" parade.

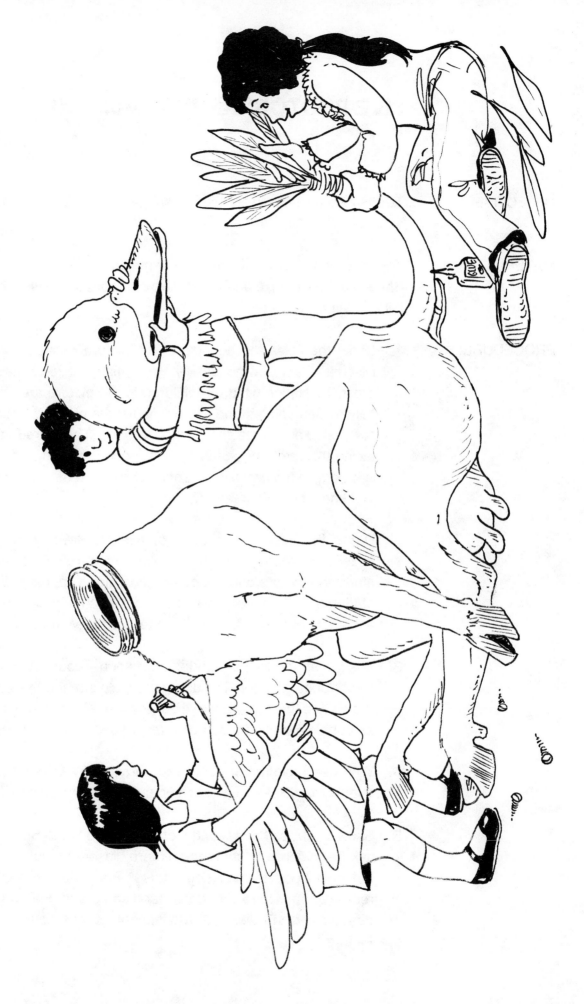

LIVE PHOTOGRAPHY - TABLEAU

OBJECTIVE: To develop a visual awareness of shape, line, color and detail in pictorial sources.

MATERIALS: The two accompanying pictures entitled "Class Picture" and "Side Show," bubble gum, a beach ball, two pompons , a cowboy hat and a duck bill and tail of feathers.

PROCEDURE:

1. Show the class the accompanying picture entitled "Class Picture." Discuss the following details: How many children have their eyes crossed? Notice what the children in the picture are doing with their hands. Can you find the sleepyhead in the picture? Notice the variety of facial expressions and angles of focus. There are four children not facing the camera - one is sleeping, one is blowing a bubble, another is looking in the opposite direction and one seems frightened. How do you know he is frightened?

2. Divide the class into groups of twelve. Have each group build a tableau (a frozen picture) of "Class Picture." Each student should study the picture and choose a character to portray. Encourage the students to study the facial expressions - the eyes, eyebrows, mouth and angle of the head. Ask them to copy the expressions and freeze.

3. Assign an additional student to each group to act as the director/photographer. The director should arrange the students so that the picture that they form is a duplicate of "Class Picture." Props such as bubble gum and a pair of wire glasses should be used.

4. When each picture or tableau is ready, take a Polaroid picture of it so that the participants can put it up against the original for a comparison.

5. Show the class the second picture entitled "Side Show." Once again ask the children to study the picture closely for not only expressions but also body shapes and angles. Encourage groups of eight to recreate the picture with body, face and props. Follow through with a director and the taking of a snapshot as was done with the "Class Picture."

Class Picture

Side Show

STORYTELLING AND STORYPLAYING

Introductory Thoughts

Part IV

Storytelling is the oldest of the speech arts. Without bubbles, bangles, and beads, the storyteller has practiced the art for centuries. As old as motherhood itself, storytelling has been bred from the unique combination of the oral tradition of handing stories down from generation to generation and the world without printing press technology.

Story selection is the first problem that every storyteller must overcome. A well selected story will have a lot of action, vivid characters, a definite plot sequence and many vocal interests including the onomatopoetic and alliterative characteristics of animal mimicry, machine sounds, crowds, street cries, and rhymes. Always make sure that the story selected matches the age-interest level of the child-audience.

The storyteller must first keep in mind that most characters in children's literature are exaggerated figures. The younger the child-audience, the more exaggerated these figures must be to communicate. Therefore, the storyteller must be concerned with those one or two outstanding characteristics that identify each figure rather than with analyzing the characters in depth and searching for their motivations. For instance, Little Red Riding Hood is best known for her naive, little girl quality. Play up these identifying characteristics vocally. Your voice needs a sweet tone, small volume, and high pitch. Furthermore, children like to hear characters talk directly to each other through dialogue. Consequently, whenever possible change indirect writing to direct discourse.

The storyteller must also be aware of the story's imagery and experience it first-hand. In other words, see, hear, taste, touch and smell everything the story describes. Actually visualize grandmother's strange physiology before saying, "But what big teeth you have, grandmother!" This technique will bring a sense of reality to the story that totally captures young listeners.

The vocal pause can be used by the storyteller to heighten the impact of the telling. Merely a space of silence, the vocal pause is a versatile and important tool. It can help to raise the level of anticipation and suspense. It can help emphasize humorous material and it can help draw attention to key words, phrases and actions. The vocal pause need not be long, but it must be placed just prior to the words and phrases you are wanting to emphasize.

The storyteller should follow the presentation with a useful conversation with the class. Questions to stimulate discussion about the theme, conflict and characters should be ready. For instance, discussion of each character's reason for being, what each character does in the story and why each character acts in certain ways would be effective. The storyteller should at all times encourage each child to draw a mental picture of each character's appearance, size and actions.

Trying on characters is the next step in the storytelling-storyplaying process. The whole class should try on each character individually or in pairs at the same time. This provides a comfortable environment without gawking class members on the sidelines. The storyteller should ask the students to walk around the room meeting and greeting others as their characters would walk making sure they capture the physical elements of the characters. Elephants would be heavy-footed whereas the gingerbread boy is nimble on his feet; giants usually have big, deep voices and baby billy goats have small voices.

During the casting of the play always ask for volunteers first. If no one raises a hand discuss the character's role once again for clarity. If no volunteer then comes forth, the storyteller can either ask someone to take on the role or take the role herself. The storyteller can include more players in any given story by either double casting it and presenting it twice or assigning students to be inanimate objects.

The final steps prior to storyplaying would include recapping the action so that all the players are positive of the sequence; physically setting the scene as to where the road, house, bazaar, etc., are located within the playing area; and handing out the necessary props and costume pieces to each cast member.

Give the players a few minutes to organize the action and run through the story. Once the play begins, the storyteller can reinforce the action from the sidelines; she can act as a narrator to bridge difficult transitions and even stop the play to remind the players of an event they missed in the sequence. However, storytellers should not get frustrated and should give positive comments even if the first playing looks unfocused and scattered. These things will improve with the playing. Remember, developmental drama **is for the participants**, not for the audience.

IDENTIFY THE EMOTION

OBJECTIVES: To encourage children to communicate feelings.

To begin storyplaying on a simple basis.

To relieve fear of going to bed through role playing.

MATERIALS: Bedsheet, blanket, pillow, toy gun, random toys, junk box of material with which monsters can decorate themselves. *There's A Nightmare In My Closet* by Mercer Mayer (Dial, 1968).

PROCEDURE: 1. Ask two children to hold a sheet in front of another student covering all all but the student's legs.

2. Student behind the sheet must communicate some emotion to the rest of the class using **ONLY** the hands.

3. After allowing a number of emotions with the hands, change to feet and legs only.

4. Discuss emotions and feelings with the children dwelling on the idea of fear.

5. Discuss with students what has frightened them at night. Tell them that it is a very common fear, but it is usually very silly. Whatever they heard or thought they saw was usually a tree blowing against a window or a shadow made by a piece of clothing.

6. Read *There's A Nightmare In My Closet* by Mercer Mayer.

7. Cast the role of the boy and cast the many monster parts.

8. Have monsters use crepe paper, ribbons, macaroni and paste, magic markers, pipe cleaners to make their bodies and faces into monsters.

9. Play the story.

THINGS THAT GO BUMP IN THE NIGHT

OBJECTIVES: To begin to develop characterizations.

To begin to develop the ability to follow a simple plot line.

MATERIALS: A twin-size sheet, a regular sheet, a queen-size sheet and a king-size sheet, (5 nightcaps are optional) and the book entitled *What Was That?* by Geda Bradley and Mathews (Golden, 1975).

PROCEDURE:

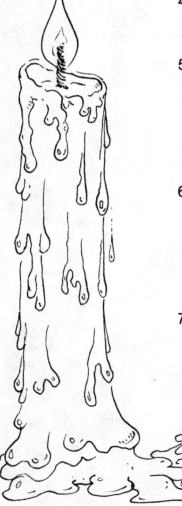

1. Discuss with the students sounds that they have heard in the night that have frightened them. Ask each student to make the sound for the rest of the class to hear.
2. Read the story entitled *What Was That?* to the class.
3. Discuss the sounds that frightened the bears.
4. Ask the whole class to think about baby bears. What shape are they? How do they move? Have the class move around the room as baby bears.
5. Cast the story: A baby bear makes his bed with the twin-size sheet, the older brother bear makes his bed with the regular sheet; the oldest brother makes his bed with the queen-size sheet and the mother and father bears use the king-size sheet. Place the beds in different parts of the room so that the bears can run from bed to bed as the sounds frighten them.
6. Cast the rest of the class as the sound chorus.
   Assign students to be responsible for:
   a. the eek, creak and squeak!
   b. a tap, rap and snap!
   c. a bump, thump and clump!
   d. all sound together as the bed comes crashing down!
7. Play the story.

MILLIONS OF CATS

OBJECTIVES:

To play a simple plot from beginning to end.

To use animal mimicry as part of characterization.

MATERIALS:

Walking stick, apron, old man's hat, newspaper, woman's knitting, two rocking chairs, if possible, and *Millions of Cats* by Wanda Gag (Coward, McCann & Geoghegan, 1928).

PROCEDURE:

1. Ask the children if anyone has a cat at home. Discussion will follow. What kind of cat? What is its name? Who has the most cats at home? Lead into the story of a woman who wanted one cat but got millions and trillions of cats!

2. Read *Millions of Cats*.

3. Discuss the story. Why did the old woman want a cat? Why did the old man bring home so many cats? Why did the cats have a fight? Why was the surviving cat not killed also?

4. Try on characters: have each child pretend he is a cat waking up, washing himself, licking up milk, purring and meowing. Divide the cats in half. One half are shy cats and the other are bold cats. The bold cats begin to walk over to the shy cats and start a fight. (Meow, hiss, scratch and run.)

5. Cast the old woman, the old man, the surviving cat, and all the rest of the cats.

6. Set the stage area: old woman and man's front porch, the hillside where cats are found, the pond where the cats drink and the grassy area where they eat.

7. Play the story.

HATS, CAPS AND HEADGEAR

OBJECTIVES: To introduce the significance of a headgear as a visual symbol.

To provide an opportunity for storyplaying.

MATERIALS: An assortment of hats, a box of craft materials such as crepe paper, ribbons, yarn, feathers, cardboard, old jewelry, artificial flowers, old greeting cards, glue and pins, *I Like Hats* by Blair Drawson (Gage Publishing, 1977) for young children K-2, *Jennie's Hat* by Ezra Keats (Harper and Row, 1966) for children in grades 3-5, *Caps For Sale* by Esphyr Slobodkina (Addison-Wesley, 1940) for all grade levels.

PROCEDURE:

1. For grade levels K-2 begin by reading *I Like Hats*. Follow this with informal conversation about the way hats help us identify community workers.

2. An assortment of hats can be displayed including such headgear as a baker's hat, a fireman's hat, a policeman's hat, a farmer's hat, a train engineer's cap, a baseball cap, a motorcyclist's helmet, a nurse's cap, etc. This assortment could include not only occupational groups but also nationalities such as a Mexican's hat, a Canadian mounty's hat, a Jewish yarmulke, a Dutch girl's cap. Ask the students to identify the caps one at a time. The class can also use the hat assortment for a lesson in categorization. For instance, ask the students to group and regroup the hats in the following categories (according to their grade level ability): first, find all the hats that identify people in sports; next, find all the hats that identify people in the health field and, finally, group together all the hats that identify a country.

3. Ask each student to select one hat from the assortment, put it on and mime what the person does who wears this hat.

4. For grade levels 3-5 begin or continue by reading *Jennie's Hat*. Discuss the many things that Jennie saw perched on top of hats. Ask the students if they can remember what Jennie used to "build" her hat.

PROCEDURE: (cont'd.)

5. Invite the students to construct hat-forms out of colored paper and then decorate them. Encourage them to use their imaginations. Be wild. Be crazy. Be colorful.

6. Read *Caps for Sale* to the students no matter what the grade level is.

7. Discuss the story. Relate the "monkey see, monkey do" proverb to the story.

8. Cast the peddler, townspeople and monkeys. Encourage the peddler to call out his "caps for sale" in loud street-cry fashion. Ask the townspeople to busy themselves with work such as gardening, digging ditches and hanging out a wash. Tell the monkeys to scurry around, scratch under their arms and squeal-laugh in true monkey form.

9. Play the story.

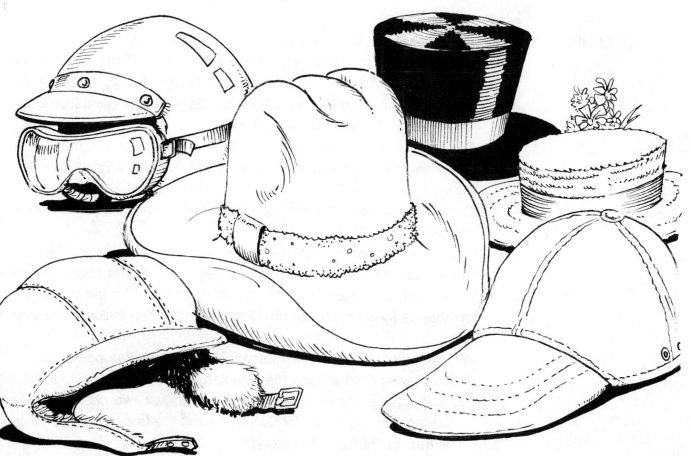

DANDELION

OBJECTIVES: To encourage children to begin or continue their work with puppets.

To encourage children to learn to follow a simple plot.

To encourage children to begin developing characterization.

To encourage children to begin developing dialogue in a creative dramatic situation.

MATERIALS: *Dandelion* by Don Freeman (Viking, 1964) and various puppet making materials. Puppet bases can be made easily with old socks. The toe is the head and the remainder of the sock, with a toilet paper tube as a neck, can be used as the body. The head can be stuffed with newspaper or cotton for shape. You may wish to cut two slits for armholes. A scrap box should be available, filled with things like materials, construction paper, buttons, ribbons, etc.

PROCEDURE:

1. Read *Dandelion* to the class.
2. Discuss things like: Why wouldn't the animals let Dandelion into the party? Do you think Dandelion looked pretty? Do you change appearance when you go special places? Do you think Dandelion learned a lesson? Do you like Dandelion?
3. Discuss the animals in the story including the kangaroo, the giraffe, and all the other animals at the party. What do these animals look like? How do they move?
4. Children may want to mime the movements of various animals being discussed.
5. Discuss a primary physical feature of each animal you plan to include in the story with the children. You may wish to add some animals depending upon the size of the class. It is helpful for the children to emphasize these dominant physical features when making their puppets.
6. Assign puppet roles. Have students construct their puppets.
7. Before having children play the complete story, you may wish to have students play some of the interactions with just two characters like Dandelion and the barber or Dandelion and the tailor.
8. Have the children play the story.

A WISE MONKEY TALE

OBJECTIVES: To encourage children to begin or continue their work with stick puppets.

To develop the ability to follow a simple plot.

To encourage children to begin expressing characterizations verbally.

MATERIALS: *A Wise Monkey Tale* by Betsy and Giulio Maestro (Crown, 1975) and various stick puppet-making materials. The puppet base should consist of either a 12 inch ruler or stick and a paper bag stuffed with newspaper. Various sized bags are recommended for various characters. The ruler or stick is placed in the bag after the bag has been stuffed and the bottom of the bag is secured to the stick with a string or yarn. A scrap box with material, construction paper, buttons, ribbons, and other odds and ends should be available.

PROCEDURE:
1. Read *A Wise Monkey Tale* to the children.
2. Discuss the following questions with the children:
   Why did the monkey fool all the animals? How did the monkey fool all the animals? Is the monkey nice? Is the monkey smart? Do you like the monkey?
3. Discuss all the jungle animals that might join the monkey in the hole. Perhaps children would like to mime the movements of some of these animals.
4. Show an example of the puppet to the class.
5. Discuss one or two distinctive features of each jungle animal with the class (zebra-stripes, lion-mane, monkey-tail, etc.).
6. Have each child select an animal to make and encourage him to emphasize the animal's distinctive features in the puppet he makes.
7. Encourage the children to play the story, telling them when a puppet talks, he **MOVES**. After children play the story once, they may wish to trade puppets and play other parts.

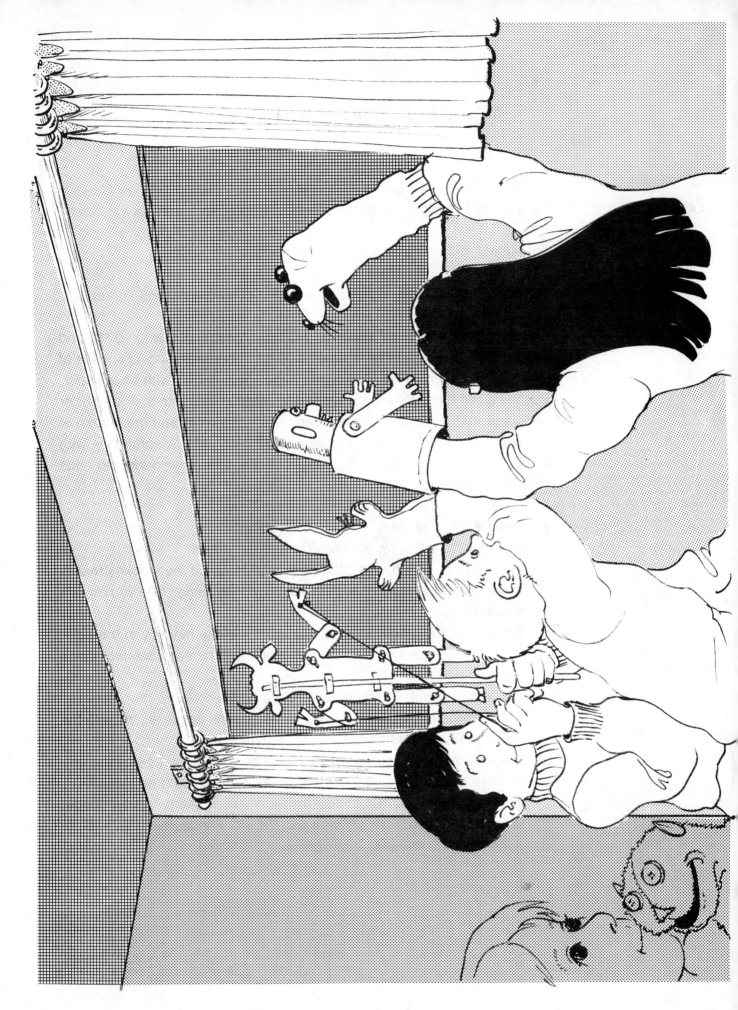

PLEASE, MOM

OBJECTIVES: To stimulate creative use of the body through movement mime.

To begin storyplaying on a simple basis through animal mimicry.

To begin storyplaying through repetitive exercises.

To encourage children to begin developing dialogue.

MATERIALS: *Can I Keep Him?* by Steven Kellogg, (The Dial Press, New York, 1971), a pet leash (optional), an apron (optional).

PROCEDURE:
1. Read *Can I Keep Him?* by Steven Kellogg.
2. Discuss children's experiences with pets and parental resistance with questions like: How many people have pets? Who would like more pets? Why do moms dislike pets? Which one of Arnold's "pets" would your mom or dad like the most or hate the most?
3. Discuss the story asking questions such as: Why do you think Arnold wanted a pet? Do you think his mom was right? How do you feel about Arnold?
4. Allow children to try the "characters." Who would like to be the dog? How would a fawn move? What would a tiger look like in someone's living room?
5. Play the story. If you wish, you might want children to be talking animals. What would a "defrosted" dinosaur say to Arnold's mom? What would a bear say if he wanted to live in someone's house?

THE GIVING TREE - TABLEAU

OBJECTIVES: To develop creative use of the body in communication.

To encourage symbolic thinking.

MATERIALS: *The Giving Tree* by Shel Silverstein (Harper and Row, 1964) and a Polaroid camera.

PROCEDURE:

1. Read the story *The Giving Tree* to the group.

2. Discuss the story on whatever level necessary to fit your group's age level. Was the little boy nice to the tree? Why did the tree always give things to the boy? Does the tree remind you of a person in a family?

3. Be sure to recap the action of the story.

4. Divide the group into units of 6 or 7 people. Have each unit work on a series of tableaux.

5. Visit each unit and help them with their pictures. Work for levels, composition, details and expressive faces as well as bodies. No props or costumes need to be used. The unit will position itself in its first picture - freeze - then move around into its second picture - freeze - then move into its third picture - freeze, etc.

6. When each unit shows its series of tableaux, the lights can be turned off as students move in and out of the tableaux and turned on only during the freeze.

7. Photographs of each picture can be taken with a Polaroid camera so that the group itself can see the tableaux.

IT COULD ALWAYS BE WORSE

OBJECTIVES: To encourage children to begin storyplaying in a non-threatening manner.

To encourage children to develop dialogue and characterizations.

To introduce children to various types of literature.

MATERIALS: *It Could Always Be Worse* by Margo Zemach (Farrar, Straus, Giroux, 1976), space large enough for children to move around freely, a record player and the record entitled "Rabbi Elimelech" available on a number of albums of traditional Jewish music.

PROCEDURE:
1. Read *It Could Always Be Worse* to the children.
2. Discuss the theme of the story. Ask questions like: Do you think the wise man was really wise? What did the old father learn? Did you like the solution to the problem?
3. Ask children to characterize several people and things in the book. What would a wise man look like, walk like? What are obnoxious children like? What would those animals act like in the house?
4. Allow several children to try various characterizations.
5. Recap the plot of the story with the group. Put the record of "Rabbi Elimelech" on for them to hear. Ask them to listen to how the units of music trace the plot exactly.
6. Divide the group in half. Encourage one half to act out the story in mime with the record and the other half to act out the story using actions and words.

"THE THREE BEARS" OPERA

OBJECTIVE: To use the singing voice by acting out a fairy tale opera style.

MATERIALS: Three bowls (large, medium, small), three chairs (large, medium, small), three benches for beds (large, medium, small), an apron for mama bear, a walking stick for papa bear, a stuffed teddy for baby bear and a long curly blonde wig for Goldilocks.

PROCEDURE:

1. Read the story of "The Three Bears."

2. Ask the students if they have ever heard their parents sing in the shower? Next ask them if they have ever sung and made up the words as they went along?

3. Sing your next question: "Do you all like the story of 'The Three Bears'?" Encourage the class as a whole to sing back to you altogether: "Yes." Sing questions and answers back and forth. Tell them that this is like an opera written in English.

4. Double cast the roles. Sing out such things as: "Who wants to be the Papa Bear" (loud and low in throat)? Ask those who raise their hands to sing back to you in loud low tones: "I want to be the Papa Bear." Then sing in medium voice: "Who wants to be Mama Bear?" Then in a tiny voice: "Who wants to be Baby Bear?"

5. Set the stage areas; the kitchen needs a table, chairs, and three bowls. The living room needs three chairs. The bedroom needs three beds.

6. Have each group of four actors (since you double cast) rehearse their opera for about fifteen minutes.

7. Play version #1 followed by version #2 for the rest of the class.

8. Recast and play until everyone has had an opportunity to sing a role.

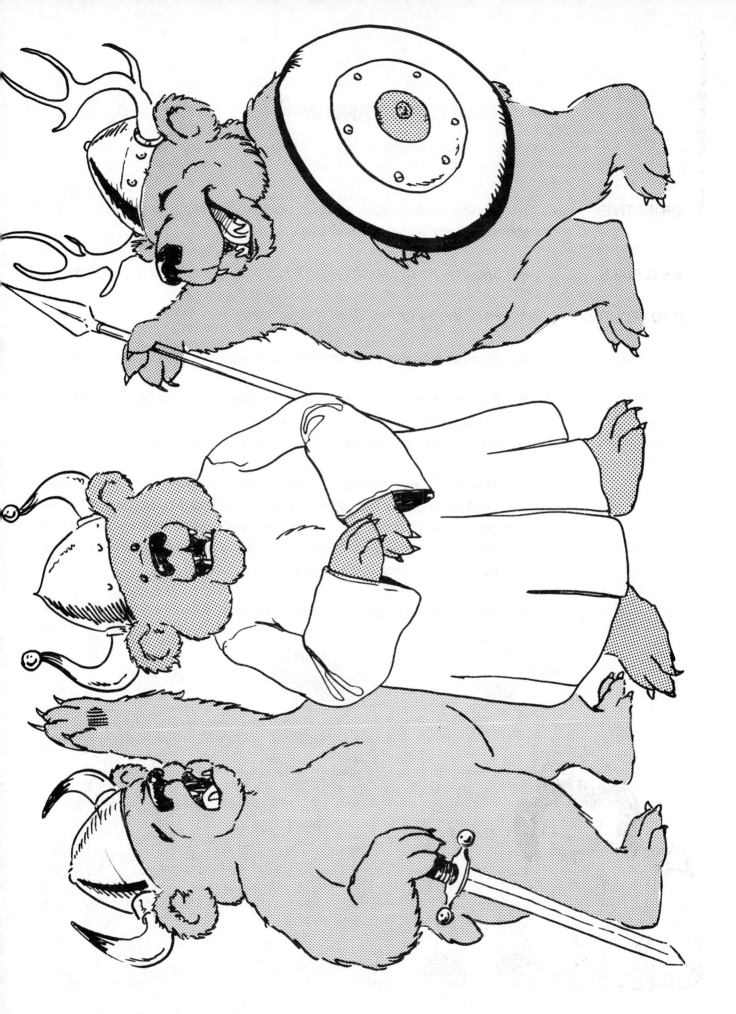

PET SHOW

OBJECTIVE: To develop each student's ability to use the imagination and respond spontaneously with body and voice.

MATERIALS: *Pet Show* by Keats (Macmillan, 1972) and blue ribbons and prizes.

PROCEDURE:

1. Read the story *Pet Show* to the class.

2. Discuss the pets each child in the story brought to the pet contest.

3. Put half of the class in pairs. Instruct them to decide who is going to be the child and who is going to be the child's pet. Strive for not just cats, dogs, birds, and gerbils but also pet spiders, pet worms, etc.

4. The rest of the class will be the panel of judges. They will ask each child as he brings the pet before the judges such questions as follows: what does your pet eat, what is your pet's name, does your pet have any special tricks? (At the same time the child portraying the pet will be using the body creatively in animal mimicry.)

5. The most clever pet will be awarded the blue ribbon by the judges.

MISS NELSON IS MISSING

OBJECTIVES: To encourage children to begin storyplaying.

To encourage children to develop dialogue and characterizations.

To introduce children to various types of literature.

MATERIALS: *Miss Nelson Is Missing* by James Marshall (Houghton-Mifflin, 1977), space large enough for children to move freely.

PROCEDURE: 1. Read *Miss Nelson Is Missing* to the children.

2. Discuss the story with the following questions. Do you like substitute teachers? Have you ever played pranks on subs? Did Miss Nelson's class learn anything? Was the detective a wise man?

3. Discuss the physical and personality differences between Miss Nelson and Miss Swamp.

4. Cast Miss Nelson and the children.

5. Have the children set up the classroom and plan their tricks and pranks.

6. Play two scenes: the first will be with a disorderly, talkative class. Miss Nelson will attempt to tell them a story. The second will be the same disorderly class but with Miss Swamp at the helm.

ONE OF "THOSE" DAYS

OBJECTIVES: To illustrate the degree to which others affect our day.

To play out scenes from the story and improvise further action.

MATERIALS: The book entitled *Alexander and the Terrible, Horrible, No Good, Very Bad Day* by Judith Viorst (Atheneum, 1972) and props listed with each scene below.

PROCEDURE:
1. Ask the students if they have ever had a very bad day where everything went wrong. Encourage everyone to contribute to the discussion.
2. Read *Alexander and the Terrible, Horrible, No Good, Very Bad Day* to the class.
3. Discuss how many small bad events can add up to a terrible day.
4. Suggest that the class play out four scenes from the book. Discuss each one separately, cast the roles, hand out the props and give each group five or ten minutes to work. Encourage each group to add further action to each scene.

SCENE ONE: *Snap, Crackle, and Pop*

SETTING: Breakfast table

PROPS: 3 boxes of cereal, 3 spoons, 3 bowls, a model car, and a code ring.

ROLES: Anthony, Nick, Alexander

ACTION:
1. Anthony finds a model car in his box.
2. Nick finds a code ring in his box.
3. Alexander finds nothing.
4. Improvise other possibilities.

SCENE TWO: *Rise and Shine*

SETTING: Bedroom

PROPS: comb, skateboard, toothbrush, an empty tube of paste

ROLES: Alexander

ACTION:
1. Alexander tries to comb his hair but he has gum in it.
2. Alexander trips on a skateboard.
3. He tries to brush his teeth but there is no paste.
4. Add more problems to this scene.

PROCEDURE: (cont'd.)

SCENE THREE:	*A Joy Ride*
SETTING:	Inside an automobile
PROPS:	school books, lunch pails
ROLES:	Becky, Audrey, Elliott, Alexander and driver
ACTION:	1. All kids pile in the car; Alex is squashed in the middle of the back seat.
	2. Alex complains that he needs a seat by the window or he will get carsick. No one listens.
	3. Alex offers to do their homework if they give him a seat by the window.
	4. Alex offers to give them bubble gum if they will give him a seat by the window.
	5. Add more action to this scene.

SCENE FOUR:	*Come and Get It!*
SETTING:	Lunchroom
PROPS:	four lunch boxes, 2 cupcakes, one Hershey bar and one jelly roll.
ROLES:	Alexander, Phillip, Albert, Paul
ACTION:	1. Phillip has 2 cupcakes in his lunch bag.
	2. Albert has a Hershey bar in his lunch bag.
	3. Paul has a jelly roll in his bag.
	4. Alexander's mother forgot to put his dessert in his bag.
	5. Improvise further action.

SILENT MOVIES

OBJECTIVE: To develop the ability to communicate via bodily action rather than voice.

MATERIALS: Silent movie props as suggested below, VTR system if available, record player and album called *Scott Joplin Rags Vol. II.*

PROCEDURE:

1. Ask the class to close their eyes and listen to "Elite Syncopations" on the *Scott Joplin Piano Rags* album and visualize a scene from a silent movie.

2. Discuss the scene that each student saw. Select three of them to work into a scenario. A possible environment for a silent movie would be a dance hall saloon. **Props:** cowboy hats, cards, dance hall girl's boa or shawl, sheriff's badge, glasses and bottles, *Cast:* sheriff, bad guy, other cowboys, bartender, dance hall girls, and sheriff's girl friend, **Scenario:** everyone playing cards, sheriff's girl friend waiting on tables, bad guy stealing something from the girl who starts to cry, the sheriff coming in and confronting the bad guy, a fight resulting with good winning out in the end.

3. Divide the class into three groups in order to develop the scenes by using only bodily action and facial expression as in silent movies.

4. Instruct part of each group to make visuals for the silent movies such as the title, any words or phrases that are keys to the action, credits, etc. A freeze-action technique is useful whenever visuals are used. A freeze-action technique requires all participants to stand statue - still while the visual is carried in front of the scene so that the audience can read it. Stop the piano music as well as the action. Work on exaggerated movement and gestures - bigger than normally used in conversation.

5. After rehearsing, have the groups share the scenes. Begin the music and enjoy the students' versions of silent movies.

PROCEDURE: (cont'd.)

    6.   Video tape the scenes if the equipment is available.

    7.   Young children could use *Flicks* by Tomie de Paola (Harcourt Brace Jovanovich, 1979) as a source for very brief silent movies.

FOURTH GRADE NOTHING

OBJECTIVES: To develop the ability to follow a plot.

To help children understand that sibling rivalry is universal.

To encourage children to develop dialogue and characterization.

To encourage children to learn to play a story.

MATERIALS: *Fourth Grade Nothing* by Judy Blume (Dell, 1972) and various props depending upon the episode you wish to re-enact. Any episode in the book is appropriate. The chapter recommended, "The TV Star," requires only a tricycle.

PROCEDURE: 1.   Read "The TV Star" or any other chapter from *Fourth Grade Nothing*.

2.   Discuss Peter Hatcher's feelings with questions like: Do you ever feel as does Peter that everyone favors your brother or sister? Does your brother or sister get more privileges than you? Have you ever been treated like a baby by some adult? Have you ever been "used" to coax your brother or sister to do something? How did you feel?

3.   Ask children to play some character pairs like Peter and Fudge, Peter and Janet, Fudgie and Janet, Mr. Hatcher and his impatient bosses, and discuss the dominant characteristics of each of these characters. Ask children to demonstrate how these pairs react to one another.

4.   Once children have had the opportunity to play one or more pairs (characters), re-enact the entire episode.

CREATIVE WRITING

Introductory Thoughts

Part V

Other than thinking, creative writing is one of the most versatile of the arts of communication. It is a non-threatening tool allowing one to step beyond the realm of self and helping one to communicate with those unseen. A story written is a one-person show presented to an invisible audience and offers children the opportunity for totally uninhibited communication.

Creativity is a uniquely human potentiality and can manifest itself in many diverse fields. The activities in this section are aimed toward developing that potential as well as offering a variety of experiences ranging from a factual "newslike" presentation to a purely imaginative escape into a fantasy world. In a world of unlimited mobility such as ours, the ability to express oneself creatively as well as effectively is an irreplaceable tool.

When beginning a creative writing project, you may have to overcome children's aversions to writing. This is possible. Story areas must be relevant to children, revolving around their interests and experiences, pets, mischief, feelings, incomplete pictures, etc. If writing topics are enriched through poetry, music, drama, or art, the student sometimes can acquire a better understanding and create with a deeper insight.

Go easy with the checking pencil. While we want to promote good writing habits and mechanics, creative writing is not necessarily the vehicle. A child will be quite reticent to express the imaginative world freely knowing it will be slashed with red. Remember, children's first written stories are articulated as they think them. They are not always planned. Spontaneity will be repressed by imposed restraints.

Creations should be shared only with the author's approval. Creative writing is a valuable tool in the classroom. It can generate tremendous enthusiasm and is a perfect road through which to enter a child's world.

DULL BEGINNING

OBJECTIVES: To encourage children to begin expressing themselves verbally.

To encourage children to use techniques of elaboration to build sentences and stories.

To encourage children to begin using descriptive speech or writing.

MATERIALS: Tape recorder, paper and pencil for each student (depending upon whether you wish to do this verbally or in writing).

PROCEDURE:
1. Teacher begins by presenting a simple sentence to the class. The dog ran away.
2. Each student must then add "color" to the sentence by adding one or two words as the sentence goes around the room.
3. This can be taped so that the students can listen to it. You may wish to write the simple sentence down and send the sheet of paper around the room in order to allow each student to make an addition.
4. When students have become adept at sentence making, you may wish to use the same idea with a story. In other words build an elaborate story from one simple sentence. *And to Think That I Saw It on Mulberry Street* by Dr. Seuss (Vanguard Press, 1937) is an excellent example of verbal elaboration. Read this story to the students and encourage them to build an elaborate scene on a street near school much like Marco did on Mulberry Street.

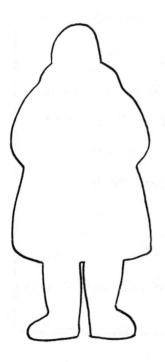

EXTRA! EXTRA! READ ALL ABOUT IT

OBJECTIVES: To familiarize students with the elements of a news story.

To develop the ability to work with words and organize thoughts from a random arrangement through a play situation.

To encourage children to begin expressing themselves through expository writing.

MATERIALS: Newspapers, scissors, paste, pencils, drawing boards, tape recorder, book of fables or fairy tales for reference, chalkboard.

PROCEDURE:

1. Discuss the elements of news stories stressing that every news story contains answers to the questions of who, what, why, when, where.

2. Divide the class into groups of three. Give each group a newspaper, scissors, pencil, glue, and poster board.

3. Ask each group to write a story by looking in the newspaper. Each who, what, why, where or when answer must come from a different story. This will allow students to create a humorous story.

4. Cut up the newspaper and paste the story together on the boards. Words and sentences that are needed but can't be found may be written with pencil. (Who, character...what, action...where, environment.. why, motive...when, time)

5. Once children have done this, take a well-known fairy tale or poem and ask children to create a news story from that. (Yesterday Humpty Dumpty, one of the king's favorite men, fell from the wall in London at 2:00. All the king's horses, etc.)

6. You may wish to have children write these stories, or you may wish to have a classroom newscast and tape it.

DELICIOUS OBSERVATIONS

OBJECTIVES: To encourage students to describe something in a sequential order.

To offer students further experience in descriptive writing.

To encourage students to describe a visual experience.

To offer students the opportunity to write persuasively.

MATERIALS: Hamburger fixings including a cooked patty, a bun, lettuce, onions, tomatoes, ketchup, mustard, cheese, pickles, mayonnaise, relish, etc., a paper and pencil for each student.

PROCEDURE:

1. Teacher asks students to watch very carefully as a hamburger is being constructed. As you construct the hamburger before the class, you may choose to be very dramatic, pulling sleeves up, wearing apron, measuring quantities of ketchup, mustard, measuring weight of meat, etc. There should be no verbal communication so that students experience **only** visual input.

2. Once the hamburger is constructed, place it on display for all to see as you give students a twofold assignment. Ask students to write a description depicting the super hamburger, while at the same time convincing their audience the sandwich is a taste-tempting, luscious treat.

3. A variation on this project might be to have a student write a recipe for the hamburger using metric measurements.

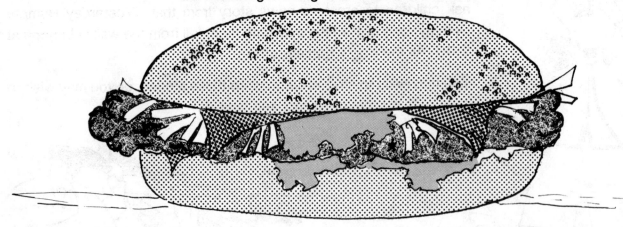

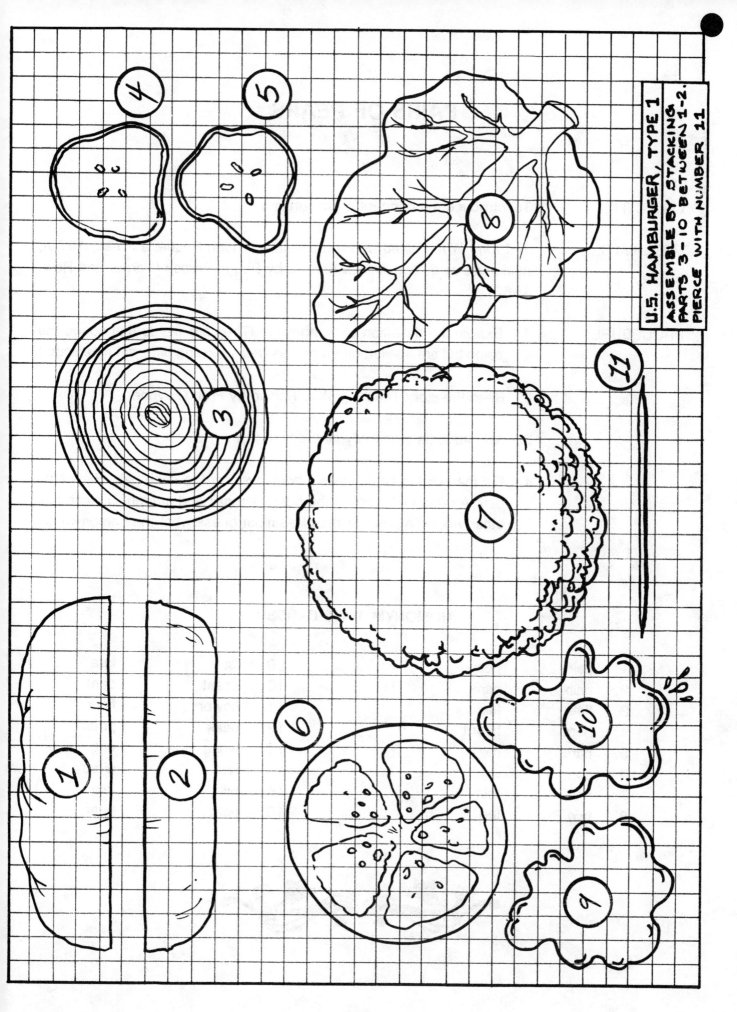

U.S. HAMBURGER, TYPE 1
ASSEMBLE BY STACKING PARTS 3-10 BETWEEN 1-2.
PIERCE WITH NUMBER 11

PAIRS OF PEARS

OBJECTIVE: To introduce the concept of homonyms.

MATERIALS: *The King Who Rained* by Fred Gwynne (Young Reader's Press, 1970), homonym cards and *Amelia Bedelia* by Peggy Parrish (Harper and Row, 1963).

PROCEDURE:

1. Explain the definition of homonyms. (They are words that sound the same but are spelled differently as well as having different meanings.)

2. Read the story *The King Who Rained* by Fred Gwynne.

3. Ask students to identify all the homonyms.

4. Put the class in pairs. Pass a homonym card to each pair. Have student A mime one word in the homonym pair and student B mime the other word. The rest of the class must guess what the homonym is.

HOMONYM PAIR CARDS

1.	pair	pear		9.	fair	fare
2.	pain	pane		10.	scent	cent
3.	flee	flea		11.	flower	flour
4.	herd	heard		12.	peak	peek
5.	hare	hair		13.	wring	ring
6.	son	sun		14.	rap	wrap
7.	rain	rein		15.	tail	tale
8.	two	too		16.	bare	bear

5. Read the story entitled *Amelia Bedelia* to the class. Ask each student to write down every homonym heard during the storytelling. After the reading see who has the longest list.

INVITATION TO A MAD TEA PARTY

OBJECTIVE: To learn the practical skills of letter writing.

MATERIALS: Pencils, lined paper, envelopes, "The Mad Tea Party" from *Alice in Wonderland* by Lewis Carroll and copies of invitations (on the following pages) addressed to each class member.

PROCEDURE: 1. Read the chapter entitled "The Mad Tea Party" from Lewis Carroll's *Alice in Wonderland.*

        2. Hand out invitations to the "Mad Tea Party" to all students. Ask them to open the invitations and study the "parts" of the letter: the address of sender, the address of the receiver, the salutation, the body of the letter, the closing and the R.S.V.P. Discuss each of these parts with the students.

        3. Ask each student to "respond very promptly" to his invitation by writing a letter of acceptance or rejection to the March Hare. Encourage the students to give reasons why they would be glad to come or are unable to attend, whatever the case may be.

August 9, 1865
March Hare
7 Lewis Carroll Lane
Wonderland, England 1865

Master David Martin
Pembroke School
Birmingham, Michigan 48008

Dear David:

You are cordially invited to a mad tea party at my home under the big tree this Sunday afternoon.

The Mad Hatter, Dormouse and Alice will all be there to share tea, bread, butter and delightful conversation. I hope you will attend. Please bring a riddle and a story.

Respectfully yours,

March Hare

R.S.V.P.

MR. WHO?

OBJECTIVES: To introduce students to the concept of a biography.

To stimulate students' imaginations.

To develop fluent thinking.

To offer students a basis for descriptive writing.

MATERIALS: The picture entitled "Mr. Who?" and pencil and paper for each student.

PROCEDURE:

1. Show the picture of Mr. Who to the class and discuss the picture with the children by asking the following questions: What does it eat? How does it dress? Who are its parents? Who does it play with? What are its hobbies?

2. Ask the class to think about Mr. Who's life. Stimulate imagination further with the following questions: Where was he born? When? What were his childhood experiences? What is his school like? Who are his friends?

3. Tell children that when we write about someone's life, we are writing a biography. Biographies can include anything from birth to a character's hopes for the future.

4. Ask the children to write a short biography about Mr. Who, using their own imaginations to "create" a life for him.

Mr. Who?

"HUGABLE" CINQUAIN

OBJECTIVES: To encourage children to begin expressing themselves in writing.

To introduce children to blank verse.

MATERIALS: *A Book of Hugs* by Dave Ross (Crowell 1980), writing paper, pencil, newsprint, and crayons.

PROCEDURE: 1.   Read *A Book of Hugs* to the class.

2.   Discuss the book with questions such as: Do you like to get hugs or give hugs? Do you have a stuffed animal you like to hug? How does it make you feel? Who in your family gives terrific hugs? Why are they terrific?

3.   Explain to the class that they are going to write cinquains about a memorable hug that they either received or gave. Explain further that the first line of a cinquain is one word long. This one word is the topic of the poem. The topic then will be "hug" on the first line of their papers.

4.   The second line is two words in length. This line describes the hug. Use adjectives here. Have them write the second line.

5.   The third line is three words long. This line tells of an action associated with the topic. Use verbs and adverbs here. Have the class write the third line.

6.   The fourth line is four words long. It is either a statement that the writer wants to make about the hug or a feeling the writer gets from the hug. Have the class write the fourth line.

PROCEDURE: (cont'd.)

7. The fifth line is a synonym for the first line. It is only one word in length. Have them all write the fifth line.

8. Share the poems. If the class is too young to write, perhaps a tape recorder could be used. The teacher could then transcribe the words to paper.

Example: (if the students wrote about themselves)

(1st line - 1 word - topic)	Me
(2nd line - 2 words - description)	smart, cute
(3rd line - 3 words - action)	always reading books
(4th line - 4 words - feeling or statement)	Likes school very much
(5th line - 1 word - synonym)	Student

ELECTRONIC HAIKU

OBJECTIVES:
To introduce children to the Japanese art form of haiku.

To discuss onomatopoeia and its use in composition.

To help children understand syllabication.

To encourage children to use their imaginations.

MATERIALS:
Small electronic toys and gadgets brought from home (radios, games, can openers, electric toothbrushes, Water Piks, game of Simon) and paper and pencil for each child.

PROCEDURE:

1. Ask children to bring some small, safe electronic appliances and games from home. **Under the teacher's supervision**, ask students to activate these games and household goods, one at a time, listening very carefully to the sounds they make. After each demonstration, have students describe what they heard. Encourage responses like buzzing, whirring, dinging, zipping.

2. Explain to the class that words that sound like the action they represent are called onomatopoetic words. Used in literature, those sounds allow readers to "hear what is going on." On the chalkboard make a class list, of all the "sound words" students can suggest.

3. Inform the students that onomatopoeia will be used with a Japanese art form called haiku. Haiku, in its pure form, is usually about nature and its wonders. It is special poetry because it is always written on three lines and can have only seventeen syllables. You may wish to review syllables with students. You may wish to read some examples of haiku to the students.

   Example:

   (5 syllables)   lazily dripping
   (7 syllables)   drops of rain quench the giant
   (5 syllables)   thirsty orange flower

4. This haiku is going to be different. The class is going to write "Electronic Haiku" (haiku about the electronic display). Write a description of the electronic gadgets students brought to school, using just seventeen syllables. Remind students that haiku is always written on three lines: five syllables in the first, seven syllables in the second, and five again in the third.

122

PROCEDURE: (cont'd.)

5. Ask each student to select one electronic item about which to compose a haiku. Encourage students to use sound words in their descriptions. When done, students may wish to share their compositions with the class.

(5 syllables)	electric mixer
(7 syllables)	is a whirring, whirling whir
(5 syllables)	whipping smooth cream white

CHAIR CHARACTERS

OBJECTIVES: To stimulate creative writing through sensory exploration of an object.

To encourage descriptive writing.

MATERIALS: Paper, pencils, chairs already in the classroom, an assortment of chairs gathered from around the school and home such as a beanbag chair, a highchair, a stool, a director's chair, an arm chair, a card table chair, a wheelchair and a rocking chair, and the poem by Theodore Roethke entitled "The Chair."

THE CHAIR

A funny thing about a Chair
You hardly even think it's there.
To know a Chair is really it,
You sometimes have to go and sit.

Theodore Roethke

"The Chair" copyright © 1950 by Theodore Roethke from THE COLLECTED POEMS OF THEODORE ROETHKE. Reprinted by permission of Doubleday & Company, Inc.

PROCEDURE: 1.   Read the poem "The Chair" to the group. Discuss its meaning.

2.   Ask each student to select a chair from the gathered assortment. Ask each student to sit in the chair and begin to explore it visually and by touch. Does it have a wooden, a metal or fabric covering? Notice its size, shape and color. Explore the surface for scratches, drawings or graffiti.

3.   Next, ask each to give his chair a name based on its size, shape, and style. Personify the chair. Is it happy or sad? Where was it born? Was it originally part of a set? Who bought it? Was it treated well? How does it spend its day? Who sits in it?

4.   Have each student write a history of the chair in first person. Let the chair do the talking. If ideas run short go back to the visual and tactile characteristics of the chair for new information.

5.   Share the chair characters with the entire class on a volunteer basis.

Chair Characters

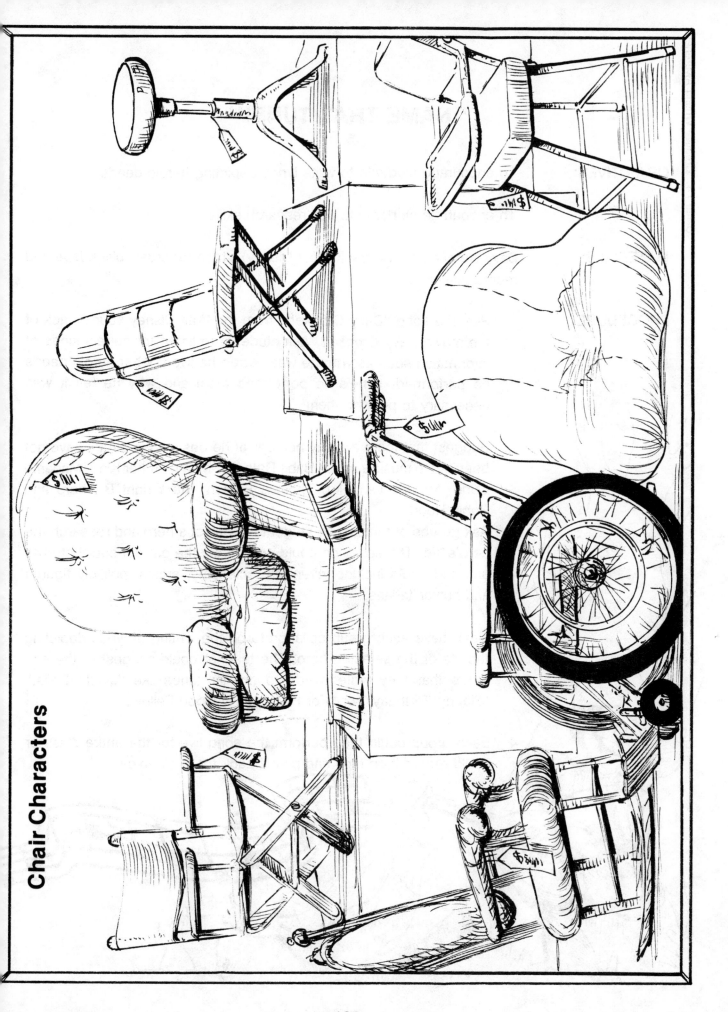

125

"NAME THAT TUNE!"

OBJECTIVES: To encourage students to write lyrics depicting heroic deeds.

To encourage students to use research skills.

MATERIALS: *Davy Crockett* sound track (Walt Disney), tape recorder, blank tape and record player.

PROCEDURE:

1. Play the song "Davy Crockett" from the Walt Disney sound track of the movie *Davy Crockett*. Ask students to listen for certain kinds of information such as **who** he was, **when** he lived, **what** heroic deeds he performed, **where** he performed them and **why** he felt it was necessary to perform them.

2. Suggest that there are any number of heroes whose deeds have not been set to music such as Babe Ruth, Dr. Martin Luther King, Madame Curie, Moses, Lancelot, Thomas Edison, the Wright Brothers and Robin Hood.
   Ask groups of four or five students to select a hero and research the hero's life. The selection could come from the current social studies unit and could include inventors, scientists, artists, political figures and humanitarians.

3. Next, have each group collaborate on the writing of lyrics depicting the life of the selected hero. The teacher could suggest to the students that they write words to familiar tunes like "Jingle Bells," "Happy Birthday," or "For He's a Jolly Good Fellow."

4. Each group could then perform the song live for the entire class or could record it on tape and play it back for all to enjoy.

KEY TO 1000 DOORS

OBJECTIVES: To encourage children to begin to write descriptively.

To encourage the use of the imagination as stimulated by visual cues.

MATERIALS: Keys of all sizes and shapes -- car keys, skeleton keys, treasure box keys, large brass keys, small silver keys, etc.

PROCEDURE:
1. Give one key to each student.

2. Ask each student to examine the key visually and think of the following questions: Is it an old key? Is it a new key? Does it look like a magic key? What kind of a door would this key open? What would be on the other side of the door? Does the key open the door of a special room, a special environment, a special historical period -- or a door to the future? What kind of door would you like it to open?

3. Ask each child to write a description of what would be on the other side of the door that the key unlocks. Feature all the details of the people, places and things on the other side.

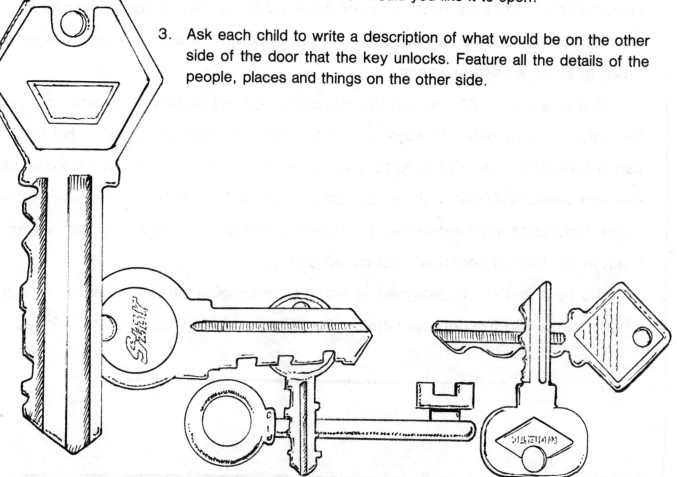

CREATIVE THINKING
Introductory Thoughts
Part VI

Throughout formal education the left side of the brain is exercised and developed by such cognitive tasks as memorizing facts, calculating numbers and reading words. The right side of the brain, however, gets little or no exercising or development. This hemisphere houses the ability to think creatively by trusting spontaneous reactions and intuitive feelings rather than logical thought.

The ability to look at one thing and see something else directs progress. New waters would never be discovered if logic was at the helm. Creative people dare to make mistakes, let their curiosity decide their investigative direction and ride their imaginations to fantastic heights never dreamed of by logic. Logical thought does not need to be discouraged, but rather, creative thought needs to be encouraged in order to strike a useful balance.

This balance would result in the educating of flexible individuals who can see the future in many different ways as well as memorize facts and figures. No longer can we afford to train a child to fit a particular occupational "slot" when grown up -------we cannot even say with any certainty what "slots" will exist in the future work force. Education must aid in the development of human beings who can act and react in the face of continual, fast-paced change.

The next section is designed to encourage imagination and inventive use of what is perceived through our senses, flexibilty in thinking and fluency of ideas.

WHO ARE YOU?

OBJECTIVE: To stimulate the use of questions as a means for gathering information.

MATERIALS: Character cards

PROCEDURE:

1. Make character cards by writing a name of a sports figure, TV personality or fairy tale character the children would know on 3 X 5 cards. The characters can be dead or alive, real or imaginary.

2. Ask for a volunteer to pick a card and pretend being the person whose name is written on the card. The volunteer will answer questions from the class by only saying yes or no. The group's first question should be an attempt to try to discover if the character is now living, male or female, real or fanciful.

CHARACTER CARDS

Cinderella	Frankenstein
The Fonz	Peter Rabbit
Joe Namath	Shirley Temple
George Washington	Superman
Rumplestiltskin	Queen Elizabeth
Santa Claus	Julius Caesar
Babe Ruth	Donny Osmond

TINKERING AROUND

OBJECTIVE: To develop the ability to put two things together in order to form a third ---the essence of creating.

MATERIALS: A huge set of Tinkertoys.

PROCEDURE:
1. Ask the class to sit in a big circle. Pour Tinkertoys in the middle of the circle.

2. Have each student go to the pile and select unrelated pieces of Tinkertoys and combine them in order to build an object --- a flower, a toy, a measuring device, a cannon, a doll, a fork, etc.

3. Ask each student to change his object into something else by magnifying it (making it larger, adding something); minifying it (taking part of it away, splitting it up); substituting a part of it; rearranging its parts; reversing it (turning it upside down); or combining it with other pieces.

**For instance a Tinkertoy sucker could become a flower by adding petals.

SHAPE COMPLETIONS

OBJECTIVE: To develop visual imagination and originality**

MATERIALS: Shape-completion sheets, pencils and the accompanying picture.

PROCEDURE:

1. Show the class the accompanying picture. Ask students to study the various geometrical shapes the artist used to create forms.

2. Take a walk around the outside of your school. Hunt for shapes -- round stones, square windows, rectangular chimneys, triangular signs, round doorknobs, marshmallow-like clouds and intricate leaf patterns.

3. Pass out the shape-completion sheets and pencils to the students. Ask students to look at each shape and make it into a picture of something. Encourage them to look at each shape and ask, "What could this shape be part of?"

4. "Three Musicians" by Picasso is a wonderful visual source for shape-completion ideas.

** Originality is determined by the unusualness of the response.

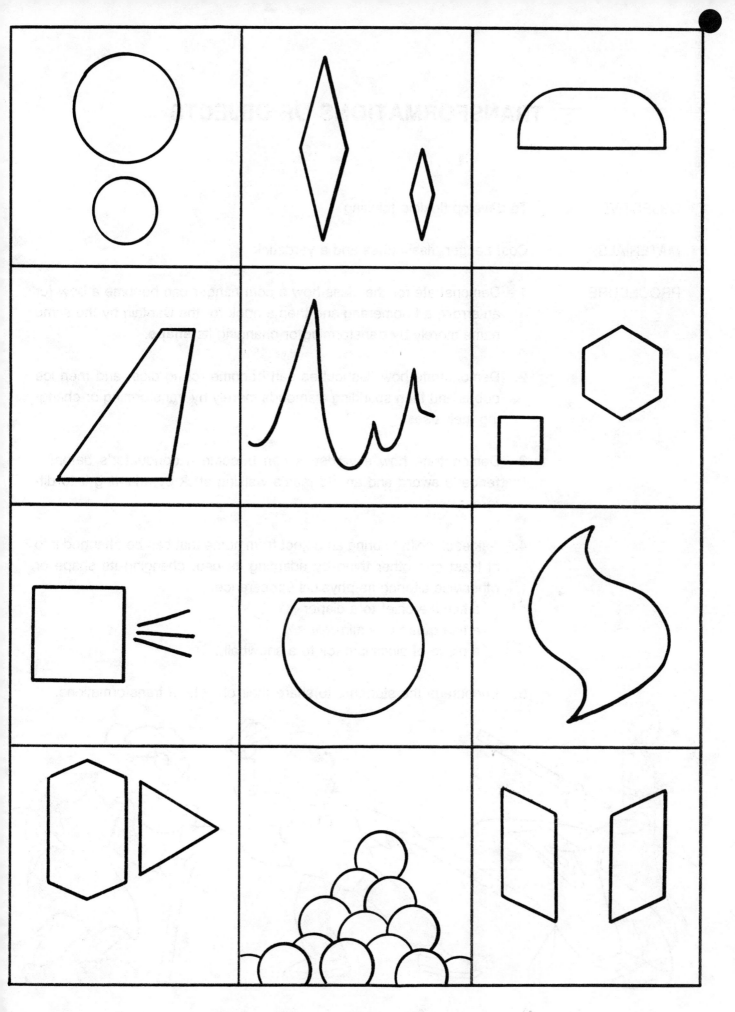

TRANSFORMATIONS OF OBJECTS

OBJECTIVE: To develop flexible thinking.

MATERIALS: Coat hanger, flashcubes and a yardstick.

PROCEDURE:

1. Demonstrate for the class how a coat hanger can become a bow for an arrow, a boomerang and then a hook for the Captain by the same name merely by transforming or changing its **shape**.

2. Demonstrate how flashcubes can become rolling dice, and then ice cubes and then sparkling diamonds merely by transforming or changing their **uses**.

3. Demonstrate how a yardstick can become a conductor's baton, a fencer's sword and an old man's walking stick by adapting it to different uses.

4. Ask each child to bring an object from home that can be changed into at least one other thing by adapting its use, changing its shape or otherwise altering its physical appearance.

    ** a handkerchief to a diaper
        a frying pan to a mirror
        a piece of aluminum foil to a snowball

5. Encourage the students to share their objects of transformations.

THE ETERNAL TRIANGLE

OBJECTIVE: To develop fluency** and flexibility.

MATERIALS: Triangle sheets and pencils

PROCEDURE:

1. Put a tray of items in front of the class and ask class members to find triangle shapes among them. The collection could include an ice-cream cone, a musical triangle, an arrowhead, a slice of pie, a witch's hat, a kite, a picture of birds flying in formation, a picture of a steeple on a church and the space inside the printed upper case letter A. The book entitled *Draw Me A Triangle* by Robyn Supraner (Simon and Schuster, 1970) is a good resource.

2. Give a triangle sheet and a pencil to each student. Ask each student to play with the triangles and make objects out of the triangles by filling them. Encourage students to "think up" as many objects as they can.

** Fluency is determined by the **number** of objects, not the quality of objects that are drawn. Flexibility is determined by the number of different categories in which the objects belong. For instance, a triangled clown's hat and a triangled pirate's hat would be two points for fluency but only one point for flexibility since they are both from "the same category."

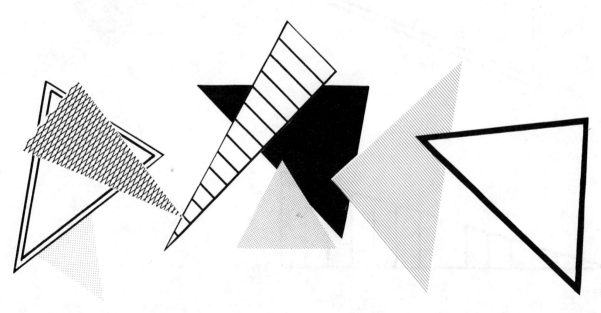

135

FACTS vs. ASSUMPTIONS OR OPINIONS

OBJECTIVE: To sharpen ability to distinguish facts from assumptions or opinions.

MATERIALS: A picture entitled "Thanksgiving Visitor," paper and pencils.

PROCEDURE:

1. Show the class the picture entitled "Thanksgiving Visitor."

2. Discuss the difference between fact and opinion. For example, "a student in the classroom is wearing blue pants" is a fact because it is undisputable. On the other hand, "this same student is wearing cool pants" is an opinion. Encourage students to give other examples of fact and opinion.

3. Ask students to write down all the facts that they see in the picture on one side of their paper and all the assumptions on the other side of the paper. Give them 5 to 10 minutes to do this. Do **not** tell them the title of this picture since there is no fact in the picture that tells it is Thanksgiving Day.

4. Discuss the facts with the group as a whole by asking for anyone to volunteer a fact. It is a fact that there is a man standing in the doorway. It is an opinion that he is part of the family. It is a fact that the clock on the wall says approximately 11:45. It is a fact that there are twelve people in the picture. It is an opinion that the little girl is the woman's granddaughter.

5. The same procedure can be followed for any picture from newspapers and magazines. If the class is too young to write the facts and opinions, the same distinctions can be drawn through verbal discussion.

Thanksgiving Visitor

IMPROVE THE SHOE

OBJECTIVE: To develop the ability to force a relationship between two unrelated objects in order to stimulate ideas.

MATERIALS: A shoe, a paper and a pencil, a forced relationship checklist.

PROCEDURE:

1. Ask each student to take off a shoe and examine its characteristics -- how does it feel, smell and look. Show the picture at the bottom of this page to the class. Ask them how the shoe has been improved.

2. Next, show a relationship between the shoe and each item on the checklist. How can a shoe be used in fishing? How can a shoe be adapted to plants? When you put a shoe and a brush together what could you get --a floor scrubber that you wear on your feet? A shoe related to socks could have spurred the idea of slippers with socks attached. A shoe related to a zipper could have spurred the idea for zip-out liners making snow boots into rain boots.

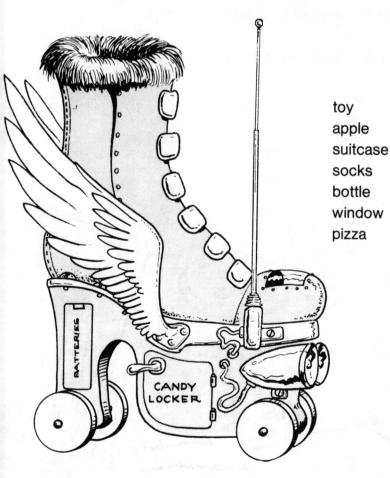

CHECKLIST:

toy	wastebasket	book
apple	comb	ketchup
suitcase	pocket	star
socks	toothbrush	ashtray
bottle	hook	bed
window	chain	dog
pizza	wheel	needle

FRANKLIN, EDISON AND ME

OBJECTIVE: To encourage inventiveness.

MATERIALS: An envelope filled with a straw, a gum ball, 4 paper clips, one 3 X 5 card, 3 small Band-Aids, 1 button, 2 safety pins and one cotton-tipped stick for each student.

PROCEDURE:

1.   Discuss with the group the various games that they own and play.

2.   Next, ask students if they would like to invent their very own games. Pass out an envelope to each student, the contents of which are the only objects that can be used in the game -- although he doesn't have to use every item in the envelope. Encourage each to examine items to see if they can be made smaller, turned inside out, upside down, made bigger by pulling together, etc.

3.   Give students twenty minutes to invent their games.

4.   Share each game by demonstrating how to play it.

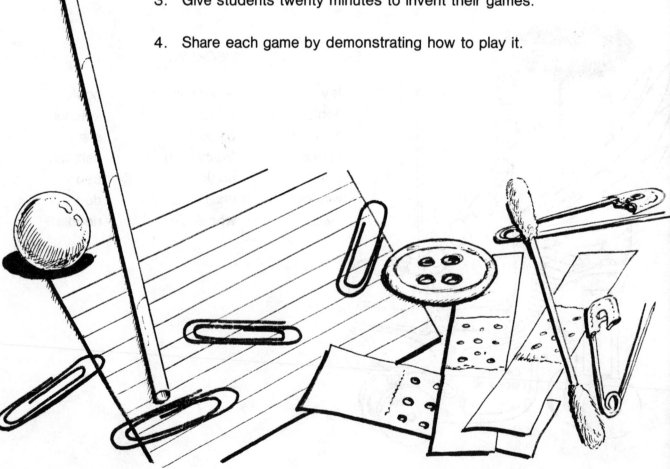

140

HOMEWORK BUBBLE INVENTIONS

OBJECTIVE: To develop inventive thinking

To develop the ability to play with problems in search of solutions.

MATERIALS: The poem entitled "Homework" by Russell Hoban, paper, pencils, drawing paper and magic markers.

PROCEDURE:

1. Read the poem "Homework" to the class.

2. Discuss with students when they usually do their homework -- after dinner, before television, as soon as school is over, etc. Ask if anyone has a special place to do homework such as the library, the living room, the basement.

3. Start a class list of all the things students don't like about homework. Write the list on the board.

4. Start another list concerning all the things the class members like to do -- eat pizza, sip Coke, have their backs rubbed, listen to music, etc.

5. Ask each student to invent a homework bubble by using the two lists. Draw a picture of the bubble. What would you put in it to make homework more fun? (Choose from your list of likes and incorporate them while studying.)

** How about a Coke machine connected to an easy chair with an automatic back scratcher! Go ahead! Play around with crazy ideas. Invent. Be silly.

6. Share each student's invention and drawing.

HOMEWORK

Homework sits on top of Sunday, squashing Sunday flat.
Homework has the smell of Monday, homework's very fat
Heavy books and piles of paper, answers I don't know.
Sunday evening's almost finished, now I'm going to go
Do my homework in the kitchen. Maybe just a snack,
Then I'll sit right down and start as soon as I run back
For some chocolate sandwich cookies. Then I'll really do
All that homework in a minute. First I'll see what new
Show they've got on television in the living room.
Everybody's laughing there, but misery and gloom
And a full refrigerator are where I am at.
I'll just have another sandwich. Homework's very fat.

by Russell Hoban

Homework Bubble Inventions